T0067119

Views
of a SOUTHERN
BLACK MAN

HARVEY WILLIAMS JR.

authorHOUSE®

AuthorHouse™
1663 Liberty Drive
Bloomington, IN 47403
www.authorhouse.com
Phone: 1 (800) 839-8640

Published by AuthorHouse   07/14/2017

ISBN: 978-1-5049-0061-4 (sc)
ISBN: 978-1-5049-0055-3 (e)

Library of Congress Control Number: 2015903929

Print information available on the last page.

NLT
Scripture quotations marked NLT are taken from the Holy Bible, New Living Translation, copyright © 1996, 2004, 2007. Used by permission of Tyndale House Publishers, Inc. Carol Stream, Illinois 60188. All rights reserved. Website

Contents

1

MY VIEW

Before writing my first article in 2002, I took into consideration many things but first and foremost on my mind was how the public, both black and white would perceive me (I was not yet involved with the Hispanic community). Being a black man, I was concerned mainly about how black people would receive my message. I wondered if I would be perceived as an Uncle Tom or a Sellout. I finally decided that it did not matter because I could no longer ignore what I had witnessed in the black community for the past 40 years. What I saw and what I was hearing did not add up, so I decided to step out of the box and write what I perceived to be the truth. I decided that my 4-week Black History Month columns would be entitled, "My View."

I had no problem writing without bias because I viewed the enslavement and deliverance of black people in America as being the manifestation of God's power. Therefore, when I began to write, I was not angry about slavery, or past atrocities inflicted upon black people. My articles would be different than that of some of the other black writers who seem more concerned with pleasing black people than telling the truth. I would just simply tell the truth and let the chips fall where they may. In a sense, I had been given "freedom of the press" and I was going to use it, fully realizing that no freedom is really free…so I braced myself for the anticipated backlash. Prior to becoming part of the local media, I studied many teachings of the late Rev. Dr. Martin Luther King Jr. I wanted to fully comprehend the essence of each message and pass it on to those who viewed him simply as a civil rights leader, killed by an assassin's bullet in Memphis, Tennessee on April 4, 1968. Let me say this before I say any more about Dr. King. Like any other man conceived and born of a woman, he was not perfect but I do believe him to be a man sent by God. I do not worship the man…but I do believe that he was a prophet.

President Abraham Lincoln may have signed the Proclamation of Emancipation…but it was God guiding the pen on January 1, 1863. One hundred years later, President Lyndon Johnson would sign the Civil Rights Act of 1964… but it was God that caused him the restless nights that led to that historic event. On December 1, 1955, Rosa Park sat defiantly on a bus seat and refused to give it up to a white man…but it was God that hardened her heart that day. Dr. Rev. Martin Luther King Jr. shared with us in 1963 that he had a dream that all men, women and children in this nation would be judged fairly but it is the power of God… that's making that dream a reality today

These icons of American Black History did not bring about the freedom and opportunity once denied black people. They were merely the instruments of Almighty God. Dr. King has been granted a national holiday and I believe rightfully so. However, I wonder if Black America really understands the essence of his messages. We come together each year to celebrate his birthday by wearing MLK attire, marching, eating, speaking, and singing old Negro hymns. However, I can't help but wonder if maybe we're too focused on the messenger…and not enough on the message. Peace!

2

WHAT'S REALLY
GOING ON

NOTE: This chapter is a compilation of my first four articles, which were written during Black History Month 2002.

During the height of the Civil Rights Movement we were encouraged to be "Black and Proud," which was much easier said than done. It's hard to be proud when you're being beaten, jailed, and killed simply because you want to be treated like any other American. We were also encouraged to stay in school and "Not Be a Dropout" because an education would qualify us to walk through the same door as any other American. Nevertheless, we were warned that without an education, we had no case.

After Dr. Martin Luther King marched us to the door of opportunity, we stood on the outside and declared, "We

Don't Want Nobody to Give Us Nothing (open the door and we'll get it ourselves)." Well, Dr. King is gone now and the door of opportunity has opened. Not opened as wide as it should be…but it's open. Who can forget the young black man at the end of the commercial saying, "All I need is a chance?" The question today is, are we (black people) using what we have, which is an opportunity, to get what we want? What more do we need?

We live in a nation where almost everybody is given an opportunity to receive a decent education, regardless of race, creed, or color. Special provisions are made to accommodate the physical and mentally challenged so that they too might have equal opportunity in the classroom. Government grants and student loans are available to those who desire to further their education by going to college or a technical institution…providing one maintains a certain grade point average (GPA). Given these opportunities, why are so many young black men dropping out of school and into prison…while young men of other races are becoming productive members of society? Could it possibly be that we are more concerned about learning what's being taught on the football field and basketball court, than we are about what's being taught in the classroom? Let's face it, not every kid is going to be a professional athlete when he or she grows up. I'm not concerned about how high many baskets our kids sink, or how many touchdowns they score. We ought to be more concerned about our children achieving the American Dream, which is a life of personal happiness and material comfort.

So, who's responsible when black students do not receive the same level of education as others? Surely, we are not saying that we are incapable of learning what's being taught in the classroom. Some of America's greatest innovations have come from the minds of black men and women; therefore, I'm convinced that we have brilliant minds, capable of achieving anything we desire. We are strong and therefore, no one can hold us back…if we apply ourselves.

We must somehow find a way to destroy the notion that we are a lazy people who refuse to think for ourselves and work for what we want. I believe the acknowledgement of God, education, and determination is the door that leads to the black man's freedom. It's been proven over the years that no man can deny us freedom if we want to be free. So, if we must be denied an education, let's not deny ourselves. Let's take full advantage of the opportunity we have because a "chance" is all we're going to get.

It was a well-known fact that during the Civil Rights Movement, "To protect and Serve" did not include African Americans. We were beaten by the police, attacked by angry white mobs, bitten by police dogs, drenched with firemen's water hoses, and even killed by those sworn to protect and serve…as we marched towards freedom. But Dr. King continued to preach a message of "nonviolence." Not only were we out manned and outgunned, we were strangers in a foreign land and only God could help us. We were at the mercy of both God and man, as laws had been enacted to oppress us as a people. But in due time, God touched the heart of a president and commanded him to order those in authority, to leave us alone and the violence against the black man, for the most part, ceased. With new laws came protection from the white man but a new breed of violence would emerge…for which there would be no laws to protect us…from ourselves.

A few years ago, Rosa Parks, mother of the Civil Rights Movement, was assaulted in her home. The assailant was not the bus driver who had her arrested for refusing to give up her seat; nor was he the arresting officer, nor was his skin white. Ms. Parks was robbed and struck in the face by a young black man. I found it strange that this incident did not dominate the headlines, nor did any of our prominent black leaders take to the streets, crying out against crime in our community. I could not help but wonder why Ms. Parks was so vulnerable. How had she been virtually forgotten by those prominent black leaders who occasionally used her Montgomery experience to fuel their own agenda? Why was she not living in a community where she would have been less likely to be a victim of violence? Then I realized the answer to all my questions. She was black and her assailant was black. Nobody cares about black-on-black crimes…with the exception of the family and friends of the victim.

Imagine the impact we would have on crime in the black community if we placed as much emphasis on black-on-black crime, as we do white-on-black acts of violence. We seem to be conveying the message that it's acceptable for black people to violate (and annihilate) one another…we just don't want anybody else to violate us. It's been said that white-on-white crime is as prevalent in white communities as it is in the black neighborhood; the only difference being, the media does not report it. I do not believe this to be true…not for a moment. The truth of the matter is, the black community remains one of the most violence place to live in

America…second only to prison. So, how do we make our community a safer place to live?

We say what's needed most in the black community is, "*Education and not Incarceration.*" Well, that has a nice ring to it but do I really have the right to violate others because I don't have an education? The only education needed to stay out of prison is the ability to discern the difference between right and wrong. Beyond that, it's up to the individual. I believe that most people know the difference between right and wrong. We have demonstrated that we are not the salvages we were characterized as being when brought to this country in shackles. We too are capable of making good sound decisions. So, if we must go to prison…let's not send ourselves.

Dr. King believed that only through non-violence could we overcome in a society where "to protect and to serve" did not include everyone. In the midst of all the beatings, bombing, lynching, etc., most African Americans did not take up arms to defend themselves. Instead, we exercised the power of "perseverance" and "reason" to overcome the oppressor. Today, acts of violence and killings are still present in our community but the race and color of the perpetrators have changed.

What was that young black man thinking when he attacked Sister Rosa Parks in her home in 1994? Didn't he know that almost 40 years earlier this was the same woman that had started a movement that would change a nation? Did he even care? We were too busy making excuses for the violence in the black community that we forgot to protect Ms. Rosa Parks from those who did not appreciate her contribution to the Civil Rights Movement. What a shame!

The violence in our community will never go away if we continue to ignore what's really going. If it's true that all men are created equal, then it's also true that all men have the ability to choose between right and wrong. Are the acts of violence among other races in America as high as among the black race? Is it true that the media reports the majority of murder and violence in our community... and only a fraction of the same mayhem that occurs in other communities?

We complain about making up the vast majority of the prison population but who's really responsible? Just what should happen to me if I break the law? Should I be angry and break the law because justice is not applied fairly, or should I exercise more caution...knowing I'm more likely to go to prison than a white person who breaks the law? Does it make sense to continue breaking laws and going to prison? That is the question. It's true that black people still have a long way to go but before we can get reach our destination... we must first make sure we're headed in the right direction.

3

WHERE ARE WE GOING?

"If the word, "nigger" is so offensive & degrading (like some of U feeling right now), then why do we insist on keeping it alive by referring to each other as "nigga?" I'm getting calls from white parents complaining that their small children are learning this word from little black kids @ school...who probably hear it all da time @ home."

I posted the above comment on Facebook (FB) a few days ago and was somewhat disappointed when none of my FB friends "liked" it. In mind's eye, I saw them fleeing from that comment as if it was the plague. But had I posted something that would not require them to leave their comfort zone, they would have taken to it like ants on candy. I guess it just human nature to ignore the truth when it's not popular to tell or bear witness to the truth. Now, if you are not a black FB friend of mine, I understand very well why you did not "like" it (even if you wanted to) because to do so would make you a racist. Well, as promised, I'm writing about it now.

The fact that I received no support from my black FB friends caused me to wonder, where are we going as a people. It wasn't like some of my black FB friends and I have not already discussed the usage of the disgusting word, "nigga" by black people. But the difference this time was to agree "openly" would cause them to be viewed (by other African Americans) as betraying their own people. Well, I beg to differ! I view such a stand as establishing respect for our people and here's why.

I'm sure the church congregation was shocked this past Sunday when I stood up to deliver my sermon. After reading the text and giving the subject (Love & Respect Yourself), I said to them, "I ain't yo nigga. You ain't my nigga. I don't have any nigga friends. I don't want any niggas around me." I also added, "Every time I hear a black person use the word nigga this is what I hear. Yassa Massa. You sho is right. I is a nigga...just like you said I is." From that point on, I had their undivided attention. In fact, some of the youth moved from the back of the sanctuary...to the front.

Hopefully, I won't have to use this dirty, degrading, obscene word again but somebody has to take a stand and stop whispering in the dark, behind closed door, about how ignorant it is for us, the black race, to keep degrading ourselves with the word nigga. Some black parents are teaching their children that the word "nigga" is acceptable in the black community but not outside...by people of another race.

I know reading this is unpleasant to some and believe me, writing it feels worst but it has to be done because it's time we put "nigga" to rest. Other races are seldom heard, or quoted using the word openly. The media treats it as being obscene, even refusing to spell it out...even when black people use it (hopefully, this article will be an exception). It's mainly the black race that's keeping "nigga" alive in America.

The use of the word denotes a "slave mentality" and can never be cool, whether it ends with "er" or "a." The meaning is the same. Trying to make it cool is the same as trying to make manure pleasant. It is degrading, ignorant, and it stinks...regardless as to who uses it or how it's used. I was never a big user of the word but I had to "practice" not using it in a sincere effort to erase it from my vocabulary. I recently befriended a young man on FB (at a relative's request) who frequently uses the "n" word when referring to his other friends but he refers to me as, "Mr. Williams." He's neither black nor white and I really wanted to "unfriend" him but then I thought, to do so would be like putting a bandage on a very deep, infested wound. So, I just let it be.

The lady who called me about her young son using the "n" word, passed on to him by a black kid, makes me realize that this word is not going away anytime soon because not only are black people keeping it alive, we are passing it's on to other races. I guess the biggest shocker came a few weeks ago when I learned a 2-year old was trying to utter the "n" word in church...while I delivering a sermon. I don't think he was trying to call me one...but who knows.

Seriously, it was at that point that I realized something has to be done so this 2-year-old kid does not grow up with "nigga" being a part of his vocabulary. If we continue to look the other way, refusing to address some of the issues plaguing the black community, there will be no future Black History Month to celebrate because the black race will *be* history. I can't help but wonder...where are we going?

4

LOST IN AMERICA

I spent the first 35 years of my life seriously searching for an identity, trying to find myself in this great land called, "America The Beautiful." Being an African American, I had no clue as to who I was, or whom I should pattern my lifestyle and appearance after. I grew up knowing my name and that I was "colored," only to learn later that I was a Negro but knowing "who" I was would take several decades to discover.

Somewhere during the voyage between Africa and America, black people lost not only their way of life but their identity as well. We even lost our concept of "beauty" and would spend the next 400 years or so trying to find it. Along with our freedom from slavery came fear and confusion. Not only were we concerned about our survival but also how we would adorn ourselves, should we survive in the new world. The climate was different than what we were accustomed to, which made it impossible to dress as we had in our homeland; therefore, our traditional African attire became a thing of the past. This was not such a big issue with most black people because they had been born in the new world and had adapted to dressing and trying to look like white people…but we were not white. We were still colored and we were lost, so we started searching for an identity of our own.

As a child, I enjoyed watching Tarzan on TV but was ashamed of the black natives who were portrayed as little more than half naked savages. It wasn't the nudity that made me ashamed (Tarzan and Jane were also half naked), it was the black skin and the nappy hair of the natives that made me feel ashamed. When I entered my teen years, I started to take a closer look at the world around me and it soon became apparent that I was not the only colored person ashamed of my dark-skinned, nappy hair brothers portrayed on TV. As children, we would refer to one another as Africans if we wanted to start a fight, crush self-esteem, or just make someone angry. However, what we didn't realize at the time was that true Africans actually had an upper hand on us, who were colored at the time. Not only did they have a country (continent), they also knew who they were. They had culture and heritage but we only had that which we had adopted from white people. We were merely a people, lost in America…trying to find an identity.

While we were yet colored, we decided to change our physical appearance to look more like white people because we had also lost our original concept of beauty. But if we were going to be more like white people, we would first have to find a way to alter our natural God-given nappy hair. Growing up, I also noticed that some colored men straighten their nature hair by applying chemicals. Colored

15

women who did not like the idea of plaited/braided hair often used a hot comb and curlers to straighten and/or curl their natural hair. But not all colored people could afford (or knew how) to alter their nappy hair with chemicals and hot irons. But those who could were often considered more attractive than those who did not.

Realizing that chemicals and hot combs could not permanently alter the course of nature (pun intended), some colored men started wearing their hair low…but not without chemicals. After applying grease and water, they brushed their natural hair to create "waves." Many of the colored women began wearing fake, long, straighten hair woven into their own; or they simply wore short or long curly wigs. Nappy hair was unacceptable. Those who did not "fix' their hair was often the object of ridiculed in school, the community and the church. No one wanted to have nappy hair, although that's who we were. Our hair was the first visible sign that we were becoming "Whitenized," which meant the less we resembled white people, the less attractive we felt.

As we entered the 60's, we decided that we no longer wanted to be identified as "colored" people so we became Negroes…for a few years. The term "Negro" would soon lose its appeal because (I'm assuming) it was too closely associated with the word nigger; therefore, we decided that we wanted to be Black. I was a bit confused by this new "identity" because just a few years earlier, to call a colored person black was both an insult and an invitation to fight. But now we were saying, not only are we black, we're proud of it. Even though "black" was often associated with evil and wickedness, that's what we wanted. The mid-60's brought about a change in the way black people wanted to be viewed.

For over 100 years, we had struggled in our effort to not only gain civil rights and civil liberties but also to look and be like white people. Many black women and men actually bleached their dark skin in an effort to become lighter in appearance. But now we wanted to establish our own identity.

Although we had spent several decades processing and straightening our hair, at the end of the day we were still colored people, who became Negroes, who were now black people. We could not escape who we were so, we had to find our place in America. We no longer wanted to pattern our appearance after white people; therefore, in an effort to establish our own identity, we created the "African Bush." It would later be dubbed the "Afro," before being called the "Natural." But was it really natural? Not for most of us.

The objective of the Afro was to convey a message that said we were "Black and Proud." Part of the uniqueness of the Afro was the fact that white American (and most other races) could not imitate us. It was our own unique hairstyle and it represented a piece of Africa. Whenever we puffed our Afros, donned our Dashikis and strapped on our sandals, it gave us a sense of being a people. Whether we walked alone the sandy shoreline or on the city streets, it reminded us of the life we had before we became lost in America. The stroll along the shorelines of America caused us to wonder what life would have been like had we remained in Africa. It's been said that, "Home is where the heart is." Well, our heart very well may have been in African but our body was in American. Our appearance, especially our hair, would reveal to America where our heart was…or would it?

The Afro was the hairstyle chosen to restore black people to their African roots but there was just one problem. Most of us needed a hot comb to "blow out" or nappy hair; otherwise, it would not stand up and form a bush. The Afro would fall after a few hours, depending on the heat of the day and it required much "picking" to keep it standing so, the "natural" wasn't so natural after all. We desperately wanted our own identity but the Afro was too much work; therefore, we went back to the drawing board in search of another solution. But wearing our God-given natural nappy hair was not an option. While we were yet marching, being black and proud, somebody was in the lab trying to find a remedy for nappy hair and as a result, the Jheri Curl was born. It would be the cure that, since becoming free Americans, we had been searching for. This was our white knight in shiny armor…or was it?

In the mid 70's, a little-known actor may very well have contributed to black people again becoming lost in America. Although this guy was white, when he performed in the unforgettable Disco movie, we soon abandoned the Afro. This young man had dark curly hair and his Disco attire was the most notable since Elvis. I don't really know if he actually caused the extinction of the Afro or not but I do know that not long after he made his 1977 movie appearance…the Jheri Curl was born. The Afro often fell due to sweating on the disco floor so, we decided that our newfound African hairstyle…our new identity… had to go. We gave up part of our blackness in exchange for convenience when we adopted the Jheri Curl to serve as our new identity. Not only did we want to look and dance like the disco guy, we wanted to be able to comb and style our hair as he did in the movie. Not long after the movie debuted, we stopped being Black and became African Americans.

The Jheri Curl turned nappy hair into curly tresses and we were well pleased with the results. Black men and women alike formed lines at the beauty salons, as we waited our turn in the chair. Those of us who were impatient, or could not afford to pay the beautician, purchased our own Jheri Curl kit and had friends alter our nappy hair. Although the Jheri Curl was convenient, it was not without problems… nor was it cheap to maintain. After removing the plastic bag each morning (had to sleep in a bag to keep the hair moist), one had to spray the hair down with an activator, which dripped like a broken faucet throughout the day. When the hair became dirty and had to be washed, the curls would disappear and the nappy hair would resurface…but not for long. A bottle of "Snap Back" would miraculously chase away the "naps" and the curls would reappear. But after two or three months, depending on whether or not the chemicals were applied by a professionally or an amateur, the roots of Africa (no pun intended) would begin to surface and the Jheri Curl would turn into a "Scary Curl."

In the mid 80's, most African Americans abandoned the Jheri Curl, as the search for an identity started all over again. This time, the barbershop would play a vital role as African American men started to accept their natural, chemical-free nappy hair. Those who did not want to "pull their brains out" trying to comb their nappy hair, had it cut low or simply shaved their head and became like the famous black basketball player in appearance.

Trying to be Colored, Negro, Black, and now African America has not been easy, as we continue our search for an identity in the Land of Freedom. But the good news is, our women can now feel justified going to the optician and having their natural brown eyes changed to blue, green, hazel, or whatever color contact lens they choose. Moreover, they can now feel comfortable when they perm their hair, or they dye it blond. Now that we are part African and part American, it's okay for them to lengthen their short hair with long straighten weave. As for most African American men, I believe a baldhead is more so a disguise…than a symbol of identification. It is (conveniently) a perfect disguise for an already balding head. We simply shave away what we're already losing and call it a "Black Thang." The latest trend now for men is braided hair and dreadlocks…but it's probably only temporary, as we continue to search for an identity. Oh, did I mention that we are starting to be "Black" again?

I believe that to teach our youth to be black is a grave mistake because we've yet to identify what being black is. We do know that being black in America has been confusing and not very good for us. I think instead of teaching them (our children) to be black, we ought to teach them to be law-abiding, God fearing Americans because the penal system is full of young black men trying to be black.

It's been said that Christianity is a white man's religion, introduce to black people by white men who wanted to make disobedience and disloyalty a sin. Well, I don't know about all that. I just know that before I became a Christian, I too was lost in America and searching for an identity… like so many of my brothers and sisters. Christianity has certainly worked for me because I no longer have to try to figure out who I am, or what I'm supposed to be like, which brings me to my next point.

While searching for my identity in the 70's, I imitated many of the fictitious characters I saw in black movies. When I saw this leading black male actor portraying a Godfather figure in a movie, I bought a derby and a pistol because I thought that's how black men were suppose appear and conduct themselves. When I saw the leading black male actor portraying a cocaine snorting drug dealer in a movie, I purchased a Super Fly Suit, wide brim hat (could not afford the Cadillac at the time) and felt justified snorting cocaine because I thought it was black men were supposed to do. When I saw the leading black male actor portraying a pimp in a movie, I purchased a cape and wanted to exploit women (couldn't afford the ride Cadillac) because that's what I thought black men were supposed to do. However, I was too naïve at the time to take into consideration how all those fictitious black characters ended up.

We are losing far too many of our young black men and women to drugs, alcohol, sexual transmitted diseases, prison and death because they are trying to be black. Like sheep without a shepherd, they are wandering around, lost in America. Many have no positive role models in the home or community in which they live; therefore, they seek to be like the black men and women portrayed in the negative side of the music and the movie industry. They're trying to be black when being black has yet to be defined. Too many of our young black men are being brainwashed into believing that to be black one has to be a thug, which leads to violence, prison, and/or death. Far too many of our young black females think being black means being a "hoe" in appearance, preferring to be sex objects…rather than respectable young ladies. Their promiscuous behavior often results in single parenthood, sexually transmitted diseases, and/or drug addiction. Sadly, far too many of our black youths seem hopelessly brainwashed into believing they are right.

I don't mind being called black but I'm really an American. Although it's obvious that I am indeed a black man, I do not "feel" black. Instead, I feel like a man. When people see me, I want them to see an intelligent human being whose skin color just happens to be dark. Whenever I talk with people, it's one on one, mind-to-mind and not skin-to-skin…whether those people are black, white, Hispanic, etc. When I felt black, I felt inferior, not worthy to converse or interact with certain people. But now that I have become a man, I feel inferior to no one…not even the President of the United States. I think I have the ability to make people see pass my skin color and see the man inside. I have to believe like that, otherwise, I would feel inferior, or angry, or both. It was not until I enrolled in junior college during the early 80's that I realized I had the ability to do practically anything I set my mind to. However, it would take a few more years before I realized that no one owed me anything…except a chance.

It's been said that black people do not stick together (support one another) as do Hispanics and other foreigners that migrate to America. It's a common complaint amongst black people that other races come to America and quickly become business owners (of restaurants, motels, convenient stores, liquor stores, etc.,). Some say this is only possible because of the government's willingness to help them financially, while denying African Americans the same privilege. I don't really know what goes on behind "closed doors" but I do know that it's very difficult, if not impossible, for a people to accomplish anything without unity. I have witnessed black people laughing and joking about how Hispanics come to America and pack themselves into one house like sardines in a can. But when they start establishing businesses and buying up property…it's not so funny any more. I've also witnessed black people making fun of immigrants from India who share the same surname and speak broken English but when Indians become business owners, after being in America only a few years…it's not so funny anymore.

I believe black people ought to be willing to learn from other races that come to America and become successful, rather than ridicule, be angry, or envious. I realize that it's never easy accepting defeat by the visiting team, or coming in last but it happens. It all depends on how you play the game. However, in all fairness, I must say that before any race of people can stick together, there must be something to adhere too. I think it's important to note that the one thing other races coming to America have in common, is "cultural stability," which black people lack. For the past 150 years, black people have been searching for an identity lost in the annals of history…stripped away by those who tried to make beasts out of men. When other people come America, they bring with them their cultural, their way of life, their identity. They can do this because they left a country of "cultural stability" and have not been forced to adapt to another.

Black people are among the very few races that have no country in which to return. We have become much too "whitenized" and too confused to return to Africa, the land of our ancestors. Not only are we lost in America, we're stuck here. This is our home so, we have to find a way to make it work. But I think a good starting point to finding our identity is to drop the "African" and become Americans. We are not Africans and unless, or until we realize that, we will forever be lost in America.

5

THE WEDDING

After being away for almost 15 years, I returned to South Georgia in 1986 and became a minister not long after. I was amazed to see how race relations in Atkinson County had improved. People were now dating and marrying whomever they chose regardless of race, or color without fear of persecution. But within there was this innate fear that things had not really changed in Atkinson County but it was a fear that I would have to overcome...the hard way.

The boldest thing I've ever done as a Christian to date is performing an interracial marriage in Kirkland, Georgia in Atkinson County. A white co-worker approached me at work and asked if I would perform the wedding for her daughter and her black fiancé and without hesitation I said, "Yes, sure." However, no sooner than I agreed, the anxiety started to set in. Being a newly licensed minister, this not only would be my second wedding (performed), but my first "formal" wedding and I wanted it to be flawless. This alone was enough to keep me awake at night but added to the anxiety was fear. Although there had been no threats, I could not help thinking about black men that had been beaten and killed for merely looking at white women; and now we're about to have a black man marry a white woman in a small southern town...and I've agreed to perform the ceremony. Nevertheless, as a minister I had a duty to perform and backing out was not an option.

On the night of the wedding rehearsal, I said a prayer before leaving home and hoped for the best. I was calm during the rehearsal and everything went as planned. But during the drive back home I couldn't help but wonder whether or not I would be alive, "This time tomorrow." On the day of the wedding, I kissed my wife and daughter and stated, "Well, I hope I make it back." I was actually afraid to let them attend because I had (somewhat) envisioned the small church being blown up, or shot to smithereens. Nevertheless, I got in my pickup and treasured every mile of the way...as though it would be my last. When I arrived at the church, the first thing I noticed was the absence of law enforcement. Needless to say, thoughts of police arriving "too late" to protect civil rights marchers "after" they had been beaten by angry mobs were very vivid in my mind... but I had come too far to turn back now.

As the people, black and white, old and young, began filing into the small church, I notice my hands start to tremble. I began whispering to myself, "Execute. You have got to execute this wedding." The more I recited these words, the calmer I became and my hands eventually stop trembling. I then started to focus on the hands of the people entering the church to see if any were gripping a weapon.

There was no avenue of escape but if I was going to die, I at least wanted to at least see it coming. Among the people entering the church that day was an elderly white lady in a wheel chair. At that point, I began to focus on the faces in the congregation, rather than the hands and what I saw was a mixed generation of black and white people who had simply come to witness a wedding. My primary concern then shifted from my own safety to making sure the bride had the perfect wedding (I knew that grooms usually just want to get it over with but brides want a flawless wedding).

When the ceremony was over, I hugged the bride and groom and was immediately surrounded by people of both races congratulating me on a job well done. I thought to myself, "Yeah, but if only you knew."

Footnote: On April 11, 2015, this couple will celebrate their 17th anniversary.

6

A Soft Answer

While employed at a substance abuse rehabilitation center in South Florida during the latter 70's and early 80's, I would often encounter people seeking help who were filled with rage. Most had previously led productive lives but was there in a last-ditch effort to salvage what little hope for recovery remained. One of my main duties as a Crisis Intervention Counselor (CIC) was to try and understand what these people were going through; and to and make them feel important again. I also monitored their vital signs (blood pressure and pulse) at least four hours to determine what degree of withdrawal they were experiencing.

Whenever someone seeking treatment (or a free meal and a cot) pressed the entry buzzer, I was the one that greeted him or her at the door. I tried to always greet them with a smile because I understood their shame, frustration, and anger. The clientele was mostly Caucasian (white) males and to be quite honest, not everyone seeking help were happy to see me. Most were nice and cooperative but there was a small percentage that was intent on making me the target of their frustration. On two occasions, while having a bad day myself, I decided to fight fire with fire. Harsh words were exchanged, which lead to blows being exchanged.

After the second altercation, my supervisor called me into her office said, "Harvey, in this profession you cannot afford to have a bad day. You have got to rise above their [clients] level. You are the professional here. You have been placed in this [CIC] position not because it's a dirty job and nobody else wanted to do it…but because we believe that you have the ability to deal with anything that comes through that door." When I told her about the verbal abuse I'd encountered as a CIC she replied, "You can take it. It's only words. It might hurt…but you can take it." You don't have to be a nigger just because they call you one. You don't have to cuss them just because they cuss you. If you're going to help them, you have got to be nice…no matter what they say." My supervisor was white…but I knew she was right.

Although there were other occasions when clients came into the facility venting their anger and frustration, the words of my supervisor held fast. Whenever someone came in and referred to me using a racial slur, I always responded with a soft answer and as a result, I never had another physical or verbal altercation with anyone seeking help. In fact, ninety percent of the hostile clients that came for treatment afterwards ended up telling me their life story, crying and apologizing for their misguided frustration/anger. As for the other ten percent, I simply ignored their behavior and monitored their vitals hourly, as I did the nice ones.

Giving a soft answer by no means make you a weakling. In fact, it takes a strong individual to *not* retaliate verbally while being called everything except a child of God but it *can* be done. I cannot say that I have completely mastered the art of responding with a soft answer...but I know it's the right thing to do.

7

BLACK-ON-BLACK CRIME

***NOTE:** This article was written shortly after Hurricane Katrina in 2005.*

New Orleans is a city that's certainly had its share of grief, pain and sorrow over the past year. However, while watching the news, I witnessed grief, pain and sorrow of a different nature...but in the same city. Five young black teenagers in that historic city were killed during a shootout. It's reported that all five deaths were drug related. Let me inform you that today is Tuesday and this tragedy occurred on Sunday. I spent at least 15 minutes online, trying to gather facts relating to this incident but to no avail. Now, I'll be the first to admit that I'm no wiz when it comes to the computer but I can usually "Goggle" and find what I'm looking for.

When I entered, "5 Teens Killed in New Orleans" into the search engine, I got several hits but when I visited the website, I had to search through tons of other news article to get to the death of these five slain teenagers. I eventually gave up and decided that I would point out the "insignificance" of their death…as it relates to other tragedies that occur in America. Although the media captured the grief-stricken neighbors of those slain, the rest of America quickly forgot about these young men. Were they forgotten because they were black? Were they forgotten because they were (possibly) shooting it out with other drug dealers? I don't know but what I do know is after making headline news on Sunday morning, I haven't heard anything else about the killings.

Although the media did not mention the race, or color of those who killed these five young men, it's a sure bet that they were black. I saw people on the news grieving but no one was marching with signs and chanting, "No Justice, No Peace." No one was marching and chanting, "Stop the Violence." No one was marching and chanting, "No More Drugs." Last but not least, I did not see or hear of any of the nation's prominent black leaders going to New Orleans to address this tragedy. The lack of concern over the deaths of these five black teenagers seems to convey the message that it's okay if black people kill one another…we just don't want nobody else killing us.

When a noted comedian/actor shared his views regarding some of the problems in the black community, he was vilified by some of America's prominent black leaders. I sat watching and listening in total disbelief as a black panel (on TV) picked apart practically everything the comedian/actor has to say about healing in the black community. What I heard was a bunch of technical, psychological "mumbo jumbo" that amounted to nothing more than (in my opinion) justification and misplaced blame. The panel was saying, in so many words, "The drugs, murder, single parenthood, and illiteracy that's plaguing many of our black is justified, so leave us alone." How sad! It's doubtful that any of these educated professionals reside in the black communities they were defending.

Five black teens get shot down and it's because they came from poor homes and had no other recourse but to sell drugs. It's been said that when a black man robs, kills, sell and/or use drugs, it's because of what society has made him; therefore, he's justified as he does all these things as a means of coping with racism, discrimination, and the injustices inflicted upon him. I'm not so naïve as to not believe that these evils exist in America but if we continue to ignore black-on-black crime there will be no black men left to discriminate against. We will be extinct…annihilated by our own hands.

8

LET'S STAY TOGETHER

The following is an excerpt taken from a sermon delivered by the author on May 29, 2011, during the 5th Sunday Community Fellowship Service in Willacoochee, Ga.

"Tonight, I can honestly say that for the first time since we have been coming together on 5th Sundays that I am not concerned about how many people are here. I am concerned about the quality of people here…more so than I am the quantity. It is my sincere prayer and desire that God will anoint your ears so you can hear the words spoken here tonight, and that He will anoint your heart so you will be able to receive them.

Let me say first that I am very proud to be a citizen of Willacoochee. I am also proud to tell people living elsewhere that I am from Willacoochee…born and raised here. I am not ashamed to tell people that I am from the town with the funny sounding name, but this was not always true. I can remember *growing up here, thinking I would leave as soon as I was old enough because this city, like most other small southern towns at that time was heavily divided by race, color, denomination and hatred. Not even the Christians would come together in worship. Back then "black" churches and "white" churches meant just that. Black folks attended black churches and white people attended white churches. If there was a funeral in the black community, there was a section reserved in the sanctuary specifically for white mourners, or white people who had come to pay their respect.*

I can remember as a bare-footed kid, walking past some of these white churches and wondering what the "white worship services" were like inside. When I became a Christian back in 1987, I used to ride by and wish I could just go inside the community's white churches and just enjoy the service. Then as my ministry began to grow, I used to wish I could stand behind the podium of one of the white churches here in town and preach the Gospel of Christ. I had all but convinced myself that I would never be able to do any of those things in this small southern town. Not only that, but I was sure that if this Christian community ever came together as one people, in one place, at one time...It would not happen in my lifetime. But my fellow Christians, I am very proud to say this night that I was wrong.

When I extended the hand of fellowship, I found some white people and some Mexicans reaching back because they wanted to come together too. But even before this happened I had noticed a change during a black funeral service; maybe it had to do with something I'd written in the paper...I don't know...but at this funeral there was no segregated section in the sanctuary reserved for white folk.

As I look around in this place tonight, I see the GLORY of God unfolding. Here we are, assembled together in the name of Jesus Christ, with no segregated sections in this sanctuary, no segregated bathrooms, and no segregated dining hall. Brothers and Sisters, we are TOGETHER and it is my sincere desire and prayer to God that we stay together. My Christian Brothers & Sisters, we have proven that we can lay aside our petty differences and come together at least four times a year. Tonight, we serve not only as living proof that God's children can come together...but also as an example for others to follow. What we are doing here in this small southern town don't happen everywhere."

"You might be surprised to know that what we're doing here tonight don't happen in some of the larger cities. There are still those who find it hard to believe that in a small southern town, in the Deep South, blacks, whites, and Mexicans can come together. And I'm telling you that I wouldn't trade this (unity) for gold...and gold is very expensive these days. What we have here has to come from the heart. You can't buy this (togetherness). That's why I say, I'm not concerned about how many people are here tonight, I want to talk to the people that is here because although we are together now...it's important that we stay together. Now, it's time to put a little fuel on the fire because no matter how hot a fire burns, if you don't feed it, it will soon burn out. If y'all don't mind, I am going to cast a few pieces of wood on the fire...for just a few minutes.

St. Matthew 18:20 reads, "For where two or three gathers together because they are mine, I am there among them." (NLT). Now, I have believed this [verse] for a long time. Three or four years ago, we (city of Willacoochee) had a crisis occur once a year. Outsiders were overrunning our small community

35

and they were doing everything they were old enough to do. But then God touched the heart of a few local pastors and we decided, with or without police escort that we would march in protest. How many of you here tonight know that there is power in marching? You don't have to grab a gun...just march in the name of Jesus Christ and watch things move. Just two or three others pastors and I had decided that we were going bring about change by marching. On the day of the march, we looked around and we saw this mass army standing behind us, ready to march with us.

I don't know if you have noticed or not but crime is at an all-time low in Willacoochee. There's not a lot going on in Willacoochee right now. Why do you think that is? Do you think that's just by coincident? Well, I can tell you that it's not just a coincident. It's because a few people came together... and they stood together for what was right. And because we assembled ourselves together, God was right there in the midst. What you see happening here tonight, Brother Eddie and I could not have done. Brother Bill, Brother Tony, and Brother Duvall, Brother Mike...we could not do this alone. It took God, reaching down from Heaven and touching your hearts to bring you here tonight. God has said that it is time for this Christian community to come together. There are those who have tried to discourage us by refusing to be a part of what we are doing...but I tell you tonight that if God be for us...who can be against us?

1 John 4:20 reads, "If someone says, I Love God, but hates another Christian, that person is a liar; for if we don't love people we can see, how can we love God, whom we have not seen. And God himself has commanded that we must love not only him but our Christian brothers and sisters." (NLT)

If you don't mind, I would like to read this verse from the English version of the Bible. But let me say first that I think we (community Christians) are doing good by coming together in one place, at the same time to worship and praise God. However, I'm one of those people that believe "good" is not good enough. I'm always thinking that we can do better...always room for improvement. What I want is, when you leave here tonight that you go out and tell somebody else that God said... He wants us to be together.

Listen, "If a man...if a Christian man say out of his mouth, "I LOVE GOD" and if that Christian Brother hates another Christian, the Christian that said, "I love God" is a liar. Now, I didn't say that. God said that! Let me tell you that it's easy to say, "I Love You" but in Willacoochee a net has been cast and it has been drawn in. Tonight, my Brothers and Sisters, we are the catch. We see tonight what we have. I'm not trying to put anybody down...I'm just telling the truth. God has removed the excuses for the Christians in this city not coming together. This place (sanctuary) would not be big enough to hold all the community Christians...if we loved one another the way God say love. But God said if a Christian man say, "I love God" and he hates his Christian Brother, that Christian man is a liar. For he that does not love his Christian Brother, regardless of his Brother's race, his color, or denomination...

Let me tell you something, in the end denomination is not going to matter to God; race is not going to matter to God; doctrine is not going to matter to God; male or female is not going to matter to God. The only thing that's going to matter to God is whether or not you accepted His son, Jesus Christ, as Lord and Savior; and did we love one another the way God said to love one another. My friends, that's what going to count…that's the only thing that's going to count. We may as well throw these little petty differences in the trashcan because they don't matter with God. And the writer asked the question, "He who does not love his brother whom he has seen, how can he love God…whom he has not seen?" You never know whom you might be sitting next to. It might be God!

Now this is tough but I have to say it. I don't know about you but I don't have time to hate the ancestors of those who may have enslaved and mistreated my ancestors. I don't have time for that. It time to move on. I don't have time to try to figure out who is legal in this city and who is not. That's God's business. That's none of my business. I have an obligation to preach the Gospel to the poor, whether they are legal or illegal. I don't have time to justify those who choose a life of crime…rather than become law-abiding citizens. I don't have time for that. I just want to do God's will and God's will is that we love one another. And if we can love one another, we can stay together because love will keep us together.

Now I am going to close with St. Matthew 25:23. "The master said, well done, my good and faithful servant." (NLT) And I want to tell you tonight people that, that's the only thing that's going to count. Will He say, "Good and faithful servant?" Or will He say, "Depart from me…for I know you not?"

"I don't understand why people can't understand this but you can't wait until we get to Heaven to come together. We've got to do it right [down] here. We are never going to agree on everything. Pentecostal Christians don't agree on everything. Methodist Christians don't agree on everything, nor do the Baptist Christians. But there is one thing that we can all agree on and that is, God so loved this world that He gave His only begotten son, so that whosoever believeth on Him would not

perish but will have everlasting life. Somebody wrote a song a long time ago that say, "Jesus Loves the Little Children." And they went on to say, "Red and yellow, black and white...all are precious in His sight." And I want you to know tonight people, that we [Christians] all are the children of God. And we are precious in His sight...and He wants us to love one another.

Let US stay together because by doing so, the other counties, the other cities, and other states will look upon us and they are going to say, "Willacoochee has something going on...they have a secret." I don't know about you, but I'm about to believe that we are God's chosen city. I believe that! Yes, we are God's chosen city. Nine, ten, eleven miles around us, they can't seem to do what we are doing here tonight.

As I close, I want you to know that this is my heart. The 5th Sunday Community Fellowship Service is my heart. But don't do this [come together] for me...do it for you. If I can get at least one church to assemble with me on the 5th Sunday, we are going to have community service in this city...somewhere. The Bible tells us that where two or more...so we don't have to have everybody in town. Let them stay home if they want to. Let them be prejudice if they want to. You come on out...and let God bless you! Amen."

9

TALKING WITH A FRIEND

"The Rev. Dr. Martin Luther King believed that all black people deserved the same rights under the law as his white brothers based on equality but he also felt that blacks needed to educate themselves, work hard, and earn the same respect as given to his white brothers. He never preached that blacks deserved a handout because they were black, or their parents/ grandparents were slaves. You never heard him say "back in the day" or that he deserved something for nothing. He believed every individual held the keys to their own destiny and it was up to them to walk forth and obtain it."

The above is a quote by a friend, taken from a conversation she and I had regarding race relations in America. I decided to make that conversation a part of the series of articles I will be writing the next two or three weeks. I decided, with her permission, to include excerpts from the conversation… because I agree with what she had to say. Being a black man,

I can speak the truth without fear of being called a racist (Uncle Tome maybe, but not a racist) but my friend who is white cannot.

I have not yet made it to the mountaintop but I have climbed high enough to see that too many African Americans are not taking advantage of the opportunities Dr. King (and others) sacrificed their life for. We demanded that our educational institutions be integrated, only to complain a few years later that much of our black heritage and culture was lost when we were "forced" to integrate. Whenever I hear that I think, "No, we didn't just say that!" We're now demanding an apology, and even restitution for slavery but yet we continue to ignore those who openly sell the drugs that are destroying our sons, daughters, as well as the livelihood of countless black families in America. Looking down, as I'm making my way up to the mountaintop, it's very obvious to me that we cannot see the forest for the trees.

Our black males are running amok, robbing, maiming, and killing each other at an alarming rate…and we're concerned about getting an apology and/or restitution for slavery. Who's going to apologize to that mother whose son was shot down because the drug dealer lured him out of school and placed a bag of dope in his hand? Who's going to pay her restitution? Who's going to pay that mother restitution for the sneakers stolen from her dead son's feet? Why are we not demanding that these modern-day slave owners, a.k.a. drug dealers, and slayers of our young men and women pay restitution to the parent(s) and/or children of these victims? Why are we still making excuses for the people wreaking havoc on our community…while pursuing the dead (former slave owners)? Personally, I think an apology and/or restitution for slavery will bring about as much positive change in the black community as did the changing of the Georgia flag.

Black-on-black crime in America is still at an all-time high and our young black men continue to make up the vast majority of the prison population. Young black males are still the biggest killer of young black males…in spite of having a new flag. Last but not least, far too many babies are being born in Georgia without a father in the home.

No, I do not believe an apology and/or restitution for slavery will bring about positive change in the black communities of America. While the "Stars and Bars" of the Confederate Flag may have been offensive to some black people…it cannot be blamed for the problems plaguing the black community.

Friend: *"Martin Luther King Jr. was and continues to be even to this day a great man but for far more reasons (I feel) than many in the black community are willing to give him credit for. First, he was a Godly man, a gifted pastor, a great Christian and someone who walked what he taught (something we have very few of today). There are many rumors and allegations of ex-martial affairs, connection with the Black Panthers, and more but I for one do not believe that there were any affairs. As for the Black Panthers, I do know there were times that he met with numerous civil rights groups but he never condoned their violence or methods."*

Me: I don't know if Dr. King was guilty of infidelity or not, nor do I know whether or not he was connected to the Black panthers. However, what I do know is he did not come to the aid of an oppressed people on his own. Not only was he a Godsend…God was with him all the way to the grave. God does not choose men because they are perfect, He chooses them because He's God; therefore, I do not try to defend Dr. King's personal life. I am far more focused on the MESSAGE…than I am the MESSENGER.

One of Dr. King's strongest weapons in his arsenal of persuasion was his belief in non-violence. No wiretaps or bugs, authentic or altered, have ever suggested anything to the contrary. Even after being physically attacked while marching, and having his child shoved, he did not strike back. There were those within his circle who thought it was time to change his "peaceful" method for achieving civil rights but he would not be moved. I must say this before I go any further. Since the death of Dr. King, I've yet to see another genuine, sincere black leader. I've yet to see another black advocate for the welfare of black people living in America. Could it be that we no longer need one?

I believe that African Americans have reached a plateau where we no longer need anyone looking out for us. We once danced to the rhythm of not wanting anybody to give us nothing…just open up the door. Well, not only is the door open, we now have educational grants and other financial aid that's available for those who really want to walk through that door. But the truth of the matter is, there are some that are not satisfied with being led to the water. They want somebody else to take the cup, dip the water, pour it down their throat and if possible…pee for them.

We have far too many so-called "black leaders" running around crying racism, injustice and discrimination and far too few who really care. They justify our young men going to prison by saying it's because they're black…and not because they have no disregard for the law, or the rules

Harvey Williams Jr.

and regulations governing the American society. These modern-day "leaders" say our young black men cannot make enough money working a legal job to support their family, themselves, and/or pay child support; however, what they're failing to say is, they can't make enough money because they dropped out of school. But then they justify our young black males dropping out of school by saying the teacher, who is often white and female, did not give them the same attention as were given white and Hispanic male students. These leaders say the teachers felt intimidated (or sexually victimized) by black male students and therefore, did not give them the attention they needed in the classroom. Man, I've heard every excuse that can be thought up when it comes to our young black men dropping out of school… and into prison.

I believe if Dr. King were alive today his focus would not be on civil rights but rather on utilizing the rights we already have. In mind's eye, I see him marching through the black communities of America, trying to persuade our young black men and women to stay in school and get an education; so that they might be able to work along side our white brothers and sisters serving in the United States Senate, Congress, House of Representatives and even the White House. I can hear him saying to African Americans in that very distinct voice, "My brothers and sisters, with God's help, I have led you to the water…but I can't make you drink."

Friend: *"Dr. King was a man of peace. He never condoned violence, even when he saw friends and members of his cause gunned down. He believed that God would accomplish his goals in His time. He believed in righteous justice but was intelligent* *enough to know that peaceful demonstrations furthered his journey towards this goal, where violence only begets violence and comes to nothing good and in the case of the black man in the 60's - only more oppression."*

Me: There's still a lot of anger in the black community and it's not all directed toward white people. In fact, I think I can safely say that 95 percent of the violence perpetrated against African Americans…is by African Americans. I've almost run out of reasons as to why this might be happening but I have yet one final reason as to why this is might be happening, which I'll share in a few minutes. But let's look at why we "say" we're so angry. One would think it's primarily the people living in the poverty-stricken areas of the black communities that are justifying the black man's anger but it's not. It's usually the older educated African Americans who have burnt the midnight oil, studying to obtain his or her college degree…during a time when being a smart black man or woman wasn't cool…that's making excuses for and justifying black-on-black crime.

Could it be that these successful Americans are now using the new generation of African Americans to vent their pent-up anger? Most seem to remain at a safe distant by not so much as visiting many of the poverty stricken, violent sectors of the black community…except maybe to preach on Sunday. These educated black men and women are smart enough to know that Ms. Rosa Parks, the mother of the Civil Rights Movement, was attacked in the black community in which she lived, so would they…if they hang around too long. So why defend the anger and violence that occurs in many of the black communities of America by blaming white people for black-on-black crime?

With the election of President Obama, many of the black "freedom fighters" now have to find a new cause for which to fight. I'm sure that many will soon realize that the White House is still the "White" House and not the "Black" House. The arguments that *the man* is holding us back weaken tremendously on November 4, 2008, when President Obama won the presidential election...by a landslide. Nonetheless, even with having a black man in the White House, there will still be anger in the black community. Why? Before I share with you the one remaining reason I can think of as to why there's so much anger in the black community, let me share this with you.

In the mid 60's, we danced to the being black and proud but the truth of the matter is, we had very little to be proud of. We were indeed black and we wanted to be proud of who we were...but we were not. We were living in a white world, struggling to not only have the same rights as white people but also trying to be like them in appearance. Not long after dancing to being black and proud, the recording artist abandoned his Afro for "processed" straighten hair...again. Don't get me wrong, I admired this guy and think it took lots of nerve for him to record such a song during a time when black people were supposed to be afraid, rather than "proud." In fact, a black man being proud during that time could get him killed. Not long after telling black people that we should be black and proud, he not only abandoned his "natural" hair (again), he also abandoned black women. That's when I started to think that he might not be so proud after all. I started thinking he was just black and couldn't help it.

There was this young black lady on a Judge TV show a few months ago that boldly stated that she did not like black women because of their attitude. When the judge pointed out that she too was black and therefore did not like herself, she blatantly denied that she was black. After realizing that he was not going to change her mind he asked, "I bet if you could kill yourself and come back as a white person you would, wouldn't you?" She replied, without hesitation, "Yes I would." It was hilarious at the time and I admired the young lady for her frankness but then I realized that it might not be so funny after all. When I thought about how many young black ladies wear long straight and/or curly hair woven into their own natural hair; and how some become blonds and brunettes; and how some wear colored contact lens, the young lady was probably speaking what many other young black women are thinking…but not bold enough to say. Then it hit me like a ton of bricks. Could it possibly be that some black people are angry…simply because they are black?

Friend: *"I was only a little kid when MLK was alive. I was only 4 or 5 when he died. I don't remember the marches or rallies; I only know what I read in books about him. But looking back over the 40 some odd years since his death, I see the black community as a whole has come so far but there are pockets of individuals, no matter how well educated, who will always look for a free ride or easy way out and base it on the color of their skin and how their great-grandparents were treated. I'm sorry, but most people are where they are socially and economically in this country because they choose to be there. Blacks, whites and Hispanics in this country all get the same education now; are given the same opportunities to attend colleges and get the same jobs based on educations, experience,* *and skill levels. They have the same chances and the same choices as do other Americans. I hate it when faced with adversity some blacks throw up the race card and plead dumb. Sometimes I wonder if King, looking down from his mansion in the sky, wonders if he did the right thing but then I see people like you and others who have seen his "promised land" and know that he has no regrets. I just wish everyone would get what MLK was all about. The good news is, at least people in our county were not marching (in his honor) under the influence of alcohol and drugs as some have done in the past. So we're getting there, it's just a few bumps left in the road that needs to be smoothed out."*

Me: That ole Negro battle hymn about "Overcoming Someday" meant that in spite of the racism, prejudice, hatred, discrimination, etc., black Americans would one day be victorious in their fight to have and exercise the same rights as any other American. This victory could only be achieved through the power of God but it was chosen leaders such as Dr. King that has led us this far. Now that we have won some battles…we still have not yet overcome. We still have some mountains to climb but no one else can help us now. We must now overcome on our own.

We must overcome the mindset that white people owe us something because of slavery. We must overcome the ideal that welfare is a means of restitution for slavery. We must overcome the mindset that a fancy vehicle, adorned with chrome wheels and fancy paint is a sign of success. We must overcome the belief that fathering children outside of wedlock makes us men. We must overcome the belief that having a baby is the way to keep a man. We must overcome the mindset that it's more beneficial to drop out of school…

than it is to get an education. We must overcome the myth that it's better to commit crime than earn an honest day's pay by working on a farm. We must overcome the belief that we're poor simply because we're black. We must overcome the belief that we deserve to be hired, whether we're qualified for the job or not. We must overcome!

We must overcome the belief that we have to engage in illegal activities because we're black. We must overcome the mindset that it's okay to destroy the livelihood of the people living in our community by selling them drugs and killing one another. We must overcome the belief that those in the community selling drugs to our loved ones are better to us… than those who brought us to this country in chains. We overcome the belief that black-on-black crime is not as serious as white-on-black crime. We must overcome the belief that conflict can only be resolved through violent means. Finally, we must overcome the belief that our enemies are identified by their skin…rather than by their character. I think that it's time for black people to sing a new song. Instead of singing "We Shall Overcome," we might ought to be singing, "We Must Overcome." I'm starting to wonder if we will ever truly overcome. I'm not sure we even want to.

In reference to the above quote by my white friend, it's unfortunate that certain people cannot speak the truth without fear of being labeled a racist. A leading black actor on a very popular sitcom was allowed (during primetime) to refer to white people as, "honky," while a leading white actor in another very popular sitcom was, for the most part, restricted to referring to black people as "the coloreds." I think with the election of President Obama, the, "I can't succeed because I'm black" excuse is rapidly losing it's power. As for people playing dumb, especially educated and professional people, it reminds me of the time when it was safer for blacks to "play" dumb to please white people, rather than demonstrate that we are just as intelligent as anyone else. Playing dumb now is simply a convenience.

10

Banning The "N" Word

"Other people seldom, if ever, say Nigga when describing black people. They say Nigger. The "A" at the end of the word for black people means, "Acceptable" but the "ER" at the end usually mean "Emergency Room" for other people. ~ Dry Humor

Should the word "nigger" be banned in America? If so, would it be a partial ban, or would it apply to everybody, regardless of race or color? Will violators be fined, incarcerated, or given community service? Is the use of the word "nigger" really less degrading if black people use it?

Those are but a few questions that come to mind when I hear that there's a campaign in America to ban the "N" word. Not long ago, there was another similar campaign to make "Ebonics" an acceptable language for African Americans. I thought at the time that it might be a good idea…if African Americans are incapable of comprehending and speaking the English language. Thank God, somebody decided that although we have centuries of catching up to do when it come to speaking proper English, we *are* indeed capable of learning the same as any other American therefore, the idea of Ebonics faded into history. Now back to this infamous "N" word.

In the past 20 years, I have heard this word used perhaps a thousand times without incident (fighting or killing). In fact, I've heard it used among the best of friends and everyone rejoiced, as if "nigga" was used to solidify friendship among certain races…mainly African Americans, as well as some Hispanic groups. I've actually been in the company of those when, if I didn't know better, I would have thought some of the people present were named, "nigga." Seriously, there are places I've left without really knowing the real name of the people I'd visited. By the way, of the thousand times I've heard the word "nigga" used, 95 percent of the time of the time it was black people using it. White people may have invented the word but black people ratified it.

What if the use of the "N" word was declared a crime and black people continue saying it, calling it a "Black Thang?" Would that result in the courts fining more of our young black men (because that's who's really keeping it alive), thus making it even more difficult for them to support a family by legal means? As for community service, is anybody really doing that anymore? We all know that failure to do community service can, and would likely result in incarceration…unless one can afford a sharp attorney that can successfully argue that the "N" word ban should not apply to black people, I seriously doubt that's going to happen.

I find the use of the words "nigger and nigga" to be repulsive and degrading, regardless as to who uses them. I feel the same about the use of the words "dog and dawg" when referring to another human being. There was a time when I accepted the use of the "N" word, so long as it was coming from another black person. Now, I see just how ignorant I was. Other races have labeled us as being ignorant and I believe the use of the word "nigga" gives that label credence.

If we really want other people to respect us, then we must learn to respect ourselves. There is nothing good or cool about the word "nigger" or "nigga," regardless as to who uses it. White people are confused because they hear our young black men referring to one another all the time as "my nigga" and they wonder what's the big deal whenever they use it. Some have even said to me that anybody can be a nigger, depending on how one behaves. To white people "nigger" is a profanity, a cuss word but they hear all the time, "nigga" coming out of the mouth of black people all the time. I've witnessed some black people defiantly using the word in the presence of white people as if to say, "You'd better not say it." I personally do not think ignorance needs any help.

So, what's wrong with the word "nigger?" Nothing…if everybody can use it. It would then be the same as everybody becoming millionaires overnight. The dollar would simply lose its power. If everybody were allowed to say "nigger" or "nigga" then the word would simply lose its power. I view the black man's exclusive right to use this derogatory term the same as I view black-on-black crime. We don't need laws enacted to stop people from calling us "nigger." We need laws enacted to stop white people from losing their jobs when they use it…if black people are allowed to it. What you think?

For those who might be offended by me writing the word "nigger" instead of "the N word," to you I say; I was not exactly thrilled by doing so but sometimes seeing something in print has more of an impact than a verbal message. I write as I do because I believe that once we (African-Americans) see how we're degrading ourselves, there's a chance that we might stop. The word "nigger" or "nigga" should be forever banned from our vocabulary but no act of congress can accomplish that…only we can do that. We continue to get angry whenever a person that's not black uses the word to describe us but we do it to ourselves all the time. My main concern is that today's black youth is being trained to think that this word "nigga" is a "Black Thang." We have to start teaching them that the word is profane, degrading and unacceptable, the same as any other "cuss" word. I think that when we realize that this word is another form of shackles, an extension of slavery, it will fade into history. White people seem to have done a splendid job teaching their children not to use this derogatory term…at least not in public.

If I were not black, I could not write this column without being labeled a racist. Somebody would declare that I just didn't understand because I wasn't black. Well, I am indeed black and I *do* understand. I understand that it's totally unrealistic to believe that logical people, regardless of race, creed or color, are going to respect you…if you don't respect yourself. Although some black people hear and use "nigga" regularly, it's uncomfortable whenever we hear, or read *our* use of the word in the media. We seem to think it should not be publicized for everyone to witness because then we feel ignorant.

I've heard a few explanations as to why it's okay for black people to degrade themselves but not okay for others to do so and quite frankly, no explanation makes sense to me. I think we need to free ourselves "mentally" because somewhere deep in the conscience of some black people there is the belief that we are indeed, "niggas." Otherwise, we would not refer to ourselves as such. I want the word "nigga" to sting in the minds of black people…the same as the word, "nigger" when used by used by white people. Congress cannot do that. This law can only be enacted within our hearts. Peace!

11

GEORGIA: A STATE DIVIDED

A few weeks ago, I wrote about a few brushes with racism I encountered as a child that left me angry and wanting to leave the state of Georgia forever. Thirty-five years later, I'm fully persuaded that there is no geographical cure for racism, hatred, discrimination, and prejudice. Some states are just better at concealing these evils than others. Georgians have always been very open about how they feel about race relations. Who can ever forget the infamous governor who literally handed out baseball bats to crack open the heads of those who got "out of their place." Needless to say, he was referring to black people.

In all fairness, I must admit that upon my return home, after leaving on a midnight Trailways bus, I discovered a Georgia that was much different than the one I've fled some 14 years earlier. Among the first places I noticed change was in the work place. Gone were the (overt) separate rules for black and white people. To my amazement, I discovered that people, regardless of race or color, received equal pay for equal work. People also respected one another, regardless of race or color. The person wearing the hat or shirt with the Malcolm X insignia worked along side the person wearing the cap or shirt bearing the Confederate Flag (Stars & Bars). People, regardless of race or color, often took breaks together, ate together, partied together, got into trouble together, and sometimes even got fired together. The color barrier as I had known it was now, for the most part, gone

Another change I noticed upon my return to Georgia was housing. The "black" projects and the "white" projects no longer existed. These dwelling was now known simply as, "The Projects." The underprivileged were now free to live wherever they chose without threats. Senior citizens, both black and white, rode the senior citizen bus together. They sat down at the same table at the Senior Citizen Building and enjoyed arts and crafts together…and they ate together at the same table. In spite of the many things in Georgia that had changed for the better over the years, there is yet one obstacle that continues to block the path of unity among the races and that's the Georgia flag. Because of the current Confederate Flag, Georgia remains a state divided.

When I joined the Job Corps in 1970, I was sent to San Marcos, Texas for training. Whenever the guys would ask where I was from, I would lie and say Atlanta, Augusta, or Savannah, Georgia. I would not admit that I was from Willacoochee, Ga. for two reasons. First, people would always laugh and ask, "Where in the world is that? Spell that!" I would then be left struggling, trying to name the closest well-known city. Second, if you were from a small, unheard of Georgia town, you became the subject of endless

"Yassa Boss" jokes and teasing. You were also perceived as being scare of white folks, at least slightly mentally challenged, and having low of self esteem." Job Corps cadets who were from Alabama and Mississippi were also subjected to merciless taunting. Even if you were believed to be from a large city in the south, you had to "appear" thuggish or gangster; otherwise, you were likely to be forced to prove that you were not a slave.

If I could have changed the fact that I was from the state of Georgia, I certainly would have…because I was ashamed of the state's history. People just naturally associated Georgia, Alabama, and Mississippi with segregation, racism, discrimination, injustice, lynching, and other atrocities. Although Jamestown, Virginia gave birth to American slavery, conceived when 20 Africans were shipped there in 1619, is better known as the birthplace of George Washington, Thomas Jefferson, and six other U. S. presidents. Massachusetts is not known for the first colony to legalize slavery in 1641, instead, it known for Plymouth Rock, the landmark where legend has it that the Pilgrims landed in 1620. Although Texas was the last southern state to abolish slavery on June 19, 1865, almost two years after Abraham Lincoln signed the Emancipation Proclamation, the state is better known for the Alamo and the famous men who died defending the fort.

Virginia, Massachusetts, and Texas all play a major role in our Black History but somehow those states have managed to escape the stigma that continues to haunt Georgia, Alabama, and Mississippi. These states have made great strives since the "bad ole days" but only Georgia remains locked in civil unrest because we can't seem to agree on which flag should represent us. The Georgia flag has been altered three times since 1955 and it's those changes that have made us the angriest state in the nation. The reason for the changes will depend on whom you ask.

In 1956 the "stars and bars" symbol was supposedly added to the Confederate flag to commemorate the 100th anniversary of the Civil War…6 years early. However, it's alleged that the symbol added in defiance of the Brown v Board of Education Decision of 1955, in which the Supreme Court ruled that racial segregation in public school violates the Fourteenth Amendment, which guarantee equal protection; and the Fifth Amendment, which guarantees due process. The Brown v Board of Education case overturned the "separate but equal" doctrine that underpinned legal segregation in America. I have yet to witness black people displaying the Confederate Flag and I have yet to engaged in conversation (with a black person) about the flag; therefore, I do not claim to speak on behalf of black people. But if you are black, you probably wonder if the Confederate Flag represents a heart that yearns for yesterday…the days of legal segregation, beatings and/or lynching. I think we all can agree that the "Stars & Bars" is a symbol of white heritage…whether that heritage was favorable towards black people or not.

For the past two months, I have refused to read some "Letter to the Editor" (newspaper) publications but for the past two weeks, I've read them with joy. The one written last week about the Confederacy, Ossie Davis, and the Confederate Flag was very educational. There's an old saying, "It's ain't what you say, it's how you say it." Now, I can better understand why and how one can be proud of their heritage…even the Confederate Flag…and not be a bigot or racist. After reading last week's article (submitted by a white lady), I understand both sides of the Confederate Flag controversy, I no longer (impulsively) view the "Stars & Bars" as a symbol that represents racism and bigotry, hatred, and/or someone's desire place black people back in slavery…but only God knows the heart of man. To be honest, I'm not concerned about which flag represents the state of Georgia, or any other state, so long as freedom, justice and equality rings. I didn't know that Ossie Davis was a native of Georgia, definitely not a native of Cogdell, Ga., just few miles from where I live; nor did I know that he worked with Dr. King…until I read last week's article.

I want to thank the bold people of Atkinson County who, during the past two months, have given their support by encouraging me to continue writing. At one very low point, while under (verbal) attack regarding the Confederate Flag, I received a call from a white minister whom I've yet to meet. He lifted my spirit by assuring me that he had not found anything racist about anything I'd written regarding the flag. Others also encouraged me face-to-face, through "Rantin' & Ravin' (newspaper), and good old-fashioned friendliness. Although I did receive a little support from the black community, most my age (and older) seemed to have held their breath to see what would happen to "Brother Harvey" for writing about such a controversial subject. To them I say, "People will never fully know freedom until they have the faith and courage to walk out of the cell that confines them."

I want to be able to read the newspaper without having to cut out sections that might cause me to wrestle (emotionally) with love and hate…for all people. I believe the mind is the door to the heart; and I believe that if I can prevent hatred from entering into my mind, I can prevent it from trickling down into my heart. As a pastor, I teach people to love their enemies…and I lead by example. It's easy to love those who love us but the only sure way to know if you can love your enemy, you have to be tested. I'm not so naïve as to go hunting with my enemy but I'm determined not to hate anybody.

In conclusion, what I've experienced during the past two months have convinced me that hatred yet exist in Atkinson County…but love is much more abundant. The citizens, for the most part, seem to just want to get along, and move on. Again, this article is "closure" for me and I don't intend to ever again address any of the above issues. Anyone who knows me, know that I am not a racist, nor do I possess a heart filled with hatred; however, I do hate bigotry but not the bigot; I hate racism but not the racist. I'm proud to be a citizen of this state, this county, and this small town. I was born here and when I die, I want to be buried here. In the mean time, I'm going to keep on writing my articles… sharing my view with the public. Peace!

FOOTNOTE: *This editorial was written prior to Governor Sonny Perdue signing legislation creating a new state flag for Georgia on May 8, 2003.*

12

THE POWER OF TRUTH

It was only after I returned home in 1986, after living in South Florida for almost 15 years, that I accepted the fact that I had been a crack addict for the past two year. I was riding with a friend one night when she turned to me and said, "I heard you were addicted to drugs in Florida." I was astounded that anyone, especially, the hometown people, would view me as a drug addict. I started cussing and denying that I had ever been addicted to anything. I had purchased a six-pack of beer and was drinking one after another while defending my reputation and character. When I was done trying to persuade my friend that it was all a lie, she turned to me again and asked, "You drink like that all the time?" I said, "No, I'm just relaxing tonight." I then realized that she was observing my behavior, while dismissing my words, as I had done so many alcoholics years earlier.

Although we talked about many other things that night, the only thing I really heard was the word, "Addicted." There was no denying my craving for alcohol, as she had already witnessed me trying to quench an insatiable thirst in my desperate attempt to escape the present. I had counseled many alcoholics and drug addicts (before becoming a crack addict); and I had gotten high with many crack addicts; and I spent my entire week's earning on crack within a few hours but somehow, I managed to convince myself that I was different. I was not a "crack head" because I had not committed any major crimes, or sold my body to get high, as did many of the men and women with whom I got high. After hearing the truth that night, I also realized that I also had a drinking problem. I wasn't an alcoholic but I was well on my way to becoming one. Nevertheless, I continued to drink but I never again smoked crack. So, what's the essence of this story? If you want to help people, you have to tell them the truth.

You can't make them accept it but People have a tendency to create their own little world and they make their own rules as to what's true or false. Moreover, people tend to associate with people that share their views (birds of a feather) and therefore, sometimes never come into the knowledge of the truth. My friend had a college degree and a good job. She was driving and not drinking that night (I did not own a car); nor had she ever smoked crack therefore, she knew nobody in his or her right mind smokes crack… or consume alcohol like I was doing that night. That's the truth!

Today, I am very thankful that my friend did not spare my feelings by keeping silent, nor did she allow room for me to justify my addictions by blaming other people…as I talked about my many troubles. There is power in the truth but the truth has to be told if we are to help others. Now let me talk a little about the truth, and the lack of it, as it pertains to race and opportunity in America.

I'm still trying to figure out how a black man can get elected president, not once but twice, in a country seething with racism, hatred, discrimination, oppression, prejudice, and the lack of opportunity for black people. How did President Barack Obama land in the White House...while so many other black men are landing in prison? I think it might be time to focus on the truth. I can only speak from personal experience and my experience has been this. I have been successful in my every attempt to achieve whatever it is in life I want. I can honestly say that, for the most part, no one has ever hindered or discouraged me from achieving what I want to accomplish in life. So far, I have been able to pretty much write my own ticket; therefore, I can't accept the, "They holding me back" stories. I don't view myself as a black man when I'm trying to accomplish something, nor do I feel like a black man; instead, I feel like a man that's determined to get whatever it is he wants. No man has the power to hold me back because (I believe) hard work and determination moves both God and man in my favor. I think most people will agree that God is not prejudice and although man might be, I believe that one can carry his or herself in a manner (regardless of race) that demands respect. Respect is not based on whether or not an individual likes you...respect is based on how much you like yourself.

I think it's important that we teach our black children about the good, bad and ugly side of America but I think it's even more important to teach them that in spite of the past... nobody owes them anything. I don't think anyone in his or her right mind should so much as entertain the thought of receiving restitution for slavery. Every time our children hear that nonsense a seed is planted in their minds that cause many to spend unproductive years (subconsciously) waiting for a plant that's never going to be. That corrupt seed often leads to dropping out of school and into the streets, drugs, violence, single parenthood, prison and death. We must be careful as to not plant corrupt seeds into the minds of our children. Every time a child hears that he or she cannot succeed in America because of the color of their skin, 80 percent of that child's hope for success is threaten…if not altogether destroyed. Let's tell our children the truth, which is if they want to sell drugs and end up in prison, they can. But if they want to stay in school and get an education… they too can possibly end up in the White House. We must teach them that it is "their" choices that will determine where they end up in life.

Parents are responsible for the success or failure of their children. Training for success begins at home and not at school. I hear some of the special interest groups making excuses and blaming teachers for the high dropout rate among African Americans (especially black males) but nobody is talking to the parents of these children. It's up to the parents to see that their children are getting what they need to be successful. There are those who profit from racism, discrimination, prejudice, etc., and therefore, they refuse to acknowledge or tell our people the truth. When President Obama was elected in 2008, there were black leaders who were quick to point out that he was only "half" black. However, prior to 2008 it was a know fact that if a man or woman had one drop of black blood in their lineage…they were considered to be colored, Negro, or black. Now that a black man has finally made it to the White House, it's because he's not totally black. I think these black leaders should place more emphasis on the fact that President Obama finished high school and furthered his education (not to mention he came from a broken home), than trying to define his race. It's amazing how some people can not only see something but also actually reach out and touch it…and call it an illusion!

"America has the largest prison population in the world. And of the over 2 million men, women, and children who make up the incarcerated, the overwhelming majority is black. We are the most unemployed, the most caught in the unjust systems of justice, and in the gun game, we are the most hunted. The river of blood that washes the streets of our nation flows mostly from the bodies of our black children. Yet, as the great debate emerges on the question of the gun, white America discusses the constitutional issue of ownership, while no one speaks of the consequences of our racial carnage. The question is, where is the raised voice of black America? Why are we mute? Where are our [black] leaders? Our legislators? Where is the Church?"

The above is an excerpt from a noted black actor/singer/activist Acceptance Speech at the N.A.A.C.P. Image Awards, delivered Feburary 2, 2013. Here's my view.

Our black leaders seem reluctant to talk about anything that has to do with the delinquency of our children that's leading to prison and death; and as a result, they are being locked away and dying in the streets at an alarming rate. If we are to ever experience true freedom, then we must start telling our people the truth…and stop blaming other people for what we are doing to ourselves. I do not believe that prison is the tool needed to motivate our young black men and women into becoming productive members of society. I think we just need to start telling them the truth. We need to tell them that there is no excuse for dropping out of school; nor is there an excuse for not pursuing higher learning. There is no excuse for our young black men selling the drugs that rewards the "Fat Cats" of America with manisons, planes, boats, and a life of luxury…while they're rewarded only a few dollars, a fancy ride, and a few pieces of gold that leads straight into a 6x8 prison cell, constructed of steel and bricks with a door that lockes only from the outside.

Instead of telling these young black men the truth, we too often glorify them by admiring the fruits of their labor and by looking the other way, as they poison our people. Somehow, we have come to view these distrubutors of death and destruction as being victims of an unjust (American) system and by doing so, we encourage them to keep doing what they do…until they go to prison or end up dead. Many of our young black females become single mothers (and HIV positive) because we train them for failure. They are not being taught the proper way to dress and how to conduct themselves for success. As parents, we first must understand that if our daughters dress in a manner that advertises their bodies, rather than her intellect, that's exactly what they are going to sell. We need to instill in them that their greatest asset lies between their ears, which is their brain and their mind. If a young lady feels or thinks she's unattractive, chances are she's going prefer revealing clothing in an attempt to draw attention away from her face. The truth of the matter is, if she presents herself as a piece of meat…that's exactly how she's going to be perceived and treated.

In conclusion, black parents cannot reasonably blame the American system for what we are failing to do with our children, and that is train them for success. Their training, and the lack of it, begins at home. It might take a village to raise a child but the primary responsibilty lies with the parents. The truth is, nobody is going to help our children if they do not put forth an effort to help themselves. I am deeply committed to helping others but only if they demonstrate a sincere desire to help themselves, otherwise, I will only hurt myself.

13

STAN

"Blacks can't govern themselves; they are prone to violence and have no principles or values. They only seek the easy way out. The history of their behavior speaks for itself. They destroy their own communities and resort to violence at every opportunity. L.A. riots anyone? They cry and complain when they feel they are the victims of racism, but blacks are the worst racist out there. They make racist comments against others and flaunt their bigotry around as if they have succeeded in life because they are good at sports. Doesn't take much brain power to play sports. Without sports or rap music, they are just thugs with nothing. The country that is willing to give you many opportunities to work hard and get an education to succeed is now a victim of double standards that you blacks showcase…Education being the key word here. Get over yourselves, and that which happened over hundreds of years ago."

The above excerpt, taken from the comments section of Yahoo, is in response to a biased stereotypical remark made by a noted black boxer about an Asian opponent. The person making the statement does not identify himself by race…only by Stan. Well, I was angered when I read his comment because I *am* in control of my life. I am *not* proned to violence. I *never* successfully played sports. I have *never* habitually committed an unprovoked act of violence. I have *never* been a part of any riot. I *do not* blame the unacceptable behavior of nonblacks on racism. I am *not* a racist and I *do not* make racist comments. I *am* successful…inspite of not playing sports. I *do not* sing or rap and I am definitely *not* a thug…but I *do* have something. I have sense enough to know that people cannot be rightly judged based soley on race, or the color of their skin. I wanted to reply to "Stan" and give him a piece of my "dormant" thuggish mind but then I thought, "No, I am going to learn from Stan. I think I'll use his very words to make a point or two."

In all honesty, Stan and I do have something in common. For instance, I don't like it either when one race of people can make racist, or biased stereotypical remarks about another…and get away with it. Two leading black actors were known for blurting racist slurs such as "whitey" and "honky" when referring to white people…and they got away with it. As far as I know, nobody complanied and their sitcoms were among the highest ratings ever. The character portrayed by a leading white actor was also racist but he never used the word nigger (neither did Stan) on the sitcom because no way could the network have gotten away with that. However, I think he did use the term spade (and maybe coon) during the series but then again, he stereotyped all races…except the white race. The popular white sitcom ranked right along side the two black sitcoms in ratings. In fact, I am still a fan of both Fred and Archie…. but I cannot believe the late-night show host that continues to get away with all those Mexican jokes.

As for the cocky boxer that lit ole' Stan's fuse, it's not the first time he's made biased stereotyical remarks about an opponent; therefore, I don't know if it was hype or just old-fashioned ignorance. I often wonder why Muhammad Ali call Joe Frazier a Gorilla leading up to their "Thrilla In Manila" bout? It's seems okay if we degrade ourselves with derogatory terms…we just don't want anybody else doing it.

14

SO, YOU WANNA
TO BE A THUG

Let me start by saying, "It's not hard to be a thug." All you need is an imagination and determination. Spend enough time listening to gangster rap, watching gangster movies and music videos and you're likely to start thinking, "I can do that," and/or "That's what I wanna be when I grow up." And before you know it, you'll be literally dying to become a thug. For all the wannabe thugs out there, I've complied a list of qualifications that will help you reach your goal.

You'll be happy to know that you don't have to be smart to be a thug. Just stay in school until you're legally old enough to drop out. In the meantime, there's alternative school…so you won't disturb the students who's smart enough to know that thug life is a one-way ticket to nowhere. Now once you've dropped out of school, you'll need to spend the day on the corner, or under the tree (every town has a "hang-out" tree), drinking 40's and smoking dope to cope with all the injustice in America. Ask the local drug dealer if you can wash his ride (gotta work your way up, you know) and if you're lucky, he might let you risk your freedom by letting you sell a few bags of his dope.

The few dollars you manage to hustle will help you get the girl with "Bootylicious" written across the seat of her too tight short shorts. She's likely to have one or more children and no job. The child support she receives from her baby's daddy, and the welfare benefits are not enough to support her "ghetto-fabulous" lifestyle; therefore, she becomes a "sack chaser," as she exposes her body in an effort to nab the guy bearing the dope sack. Now that she has your attention, you have to move into the government subsided housing with her and stake your claim by giving her another baby, or two. That way, you prove to your "homies" that she belongs to you and that you're indeed the man of that castle... although it's really the taxpayers keeping a roof over your head and affording the rent-to-own 50" flat screen TV you and your lady watching.

In the mean time, you've done well with the few bags of dope entrusted to you by the local drug dealer and now it's time to get you a ride, but not just any ride. Buy yourself a $300 car and slap on a set of $3,000 wheels. Then install a $1,500 boom box inside and you're on your way, man. Oh yeah, and don't forget to put some of that fabulous fake fool's gold in your mouth because when you flash that big grin, you want other to think that the glitter is real. Now, the boys are really starting to look up to you. In fact, you've started to let them sling a few bags of dope for you. Just look at you. Only a few weeks of on-the-job training and already you are a mentor…training others to go to prison, or get killed.

Although you're on your way up, the more gangster videos you watch and listen to, the more you realize that you're still small fry; therefore, you gotta think of ways to boast your image in the community. Your addiction to "bling-bling" and flashy vehicles will simply not allow you to appear as a law-abiding citizen, investing in legitimate businesses, as do your pimp…I mean supplier. Your addiction thugism demands that you announce to the world, "Hey, look at me. I'm on my way to prison."

Now, to be a bone fide thug, you have to gain a reputation for being tough. You gotta have a "9" (legal or not) and the people around you have to know that you have it and that you're not afraid to use it. In fact, you can hardly wait to show them that you ain't playing about your money. You don't really wanna "pop" nobody but you got to because you can't appear soft by letting people mess you around. After all, your pimp…I mean dealer…is depending on you to make his money so he can maintain his lavish lifestyle, as he's starting to become anonymous. Also, if you really want to be a thug, and not just in appearance only, you gotta get shot or stabbed because you must have battle scars to be legit; and if you're really, really serious, you need to get shot, not just once but several times…as did some of the other now deceased gangster rappers. If you're lucky, you will live to boast about how many times you were shot.

Your reputation has now begun to flourish, as you turn out more little wannabe thugs to handle your dope. They look up to you but don't realize that you too are being pimped…I mean working for somebody. You instruct them well, telling them to sell only to the people they know, as you turn them loose them upon your own community…to destroy the livelihood of your own people. In the meantime, you continue to blame others for the lack of progress and/or success in the black community. Of course, it's only a smoke screen because you are the one that's holding your people back. But sooner or later, one of your little wannabes is going to get greedy and sell to the wrong person; or he's going to violate his probation and get taken down for an interview. The interviewers are not really interested in him…it's you they want.

During the interrogation, the wannabe thug remains loyal (to you) until given the choice of going home or going to prison. Guess which one he's going to choose. Suddenly, he realizes that it's "your" dope he's selling and you're the one with the pretty girl in government housing. You're the one that has the pimped-out ride, while he's the one walking and taking all the risks. He just decided that he's not about to go down for you. In fact, he's tired of being your "boy" anyway and with you gone, there's a chance he might become the "man." After all, you know there's no honor among thieves.

Prison is the place where you will either earn your G.E.D. or receive a diploma in thuggism, or continue to be pimped…but in a different manner. If you're not man enough to pass the thug test on the street, you can simply get a legitimate job and forget about it; but if you fail the thug test in prison, chances are you'll end up "under" somebody's wings for protection…for a price. What price are you willing to pay?

Now that you've done your time, you don't want the boys to think you're soft. Hopefully, no one in the community will ever know the price you paid for protection while in prison. Nevertheless, if you're lucky, one of the wannabes you mentored might toss you a few bags to help you back on your feet. You never realize that he's the one that "flipped" on you during the interview, because you're not very smart. Remember? Holding onto your dream of becoming a thug, you're back on the streets trying to work your way back up. In the meantime, you're just hoping somebody will mess with you because you're still angry about being "protected" in prison. You've got to convince yourself that you're still a man, in spite of what happened to you. If you're really, really lucky, this time instead of needing "protection," you're end up on Death Row. There you can learn how read and write so you can a write book about your life story, explaining how you became a thug. So now you see, from beginning to end, how to be a thug. It's not hard at all. You really don't have to be smart…if you REALLY wannabe a thug.

15

I AM NOT ANGRY

I thank God for allowing me to live in the greatest country on the face of the earth, even though the journey here was not without blood, sweat and tears. As a young man in the late 70's and early 80's, I looked for reasons to be angry for being black in America but I found none. I could never bring myself to be angry about the enslavement of my ancestors and today, I teach others not to be angry as well. I view anger, fueled by the past, as another form of bondage. As long as the mind is enslaved...so is the body.

I live in a country where I am free to not only speak my mind but also have my thoughts published without fear of repercussions. No, it wasn't always like this, but it is now. I am free to openly read and learn from any book I choose. My education is not limited by the lack of money and I can sit in the same classroom as others and learn from the same instructor as any other American. Moreover, with the proper education, I can become an instructor and teach students regardless of their race, creed or color. I can even become an overseer and instructor of instructors…so why should I be angry?

I'm not angry about the high unemployment rate among young black men, any more so than I am about the [high school] dropout rate among young black males. I'm not angry because we are far past the days when black males in America had to dropout of school to help support the family. Dropping out of school today is a choice therefore, I am not angry that young black men make up the vast majority of the American prison population, especially, when they go to jail for committing crime. They make conscience decisions to be "pimped" by those who actually own the drugs that are destroying black America. Black men do not own the boats and planes necessary to import the drugs that continue to enslave black people in America. Some black leaders are so blinded by angry (because of slavery and other atrocities) that they cannot see what's happening with our young black men…or they're just not addressing it. Some actually feast off injustice.

I'm not angry when a white man kills an innocent black man, any more so than when a black man kills an innocent black man. Black men are to be the biggest killer of black men, so why should I be angry when a white man kills a black man. Some say the killing of black men by other black men is orchestrated by a great white conspiracy but I give black people more credit than that. I don't think we are so naïve as to allow ourselves to be manipulated to the point of extinction…and that's exactly where we're headed…if we don't stop killing one another.

I'm not angry that my ancestors were brought to America as slaves, nor am I angry with the ancestors of those who brought them here. I have seen many of the gruesome images of black men, women, and children tortured, maimed and killed by evil men but yet, I am not angry. In spite of everything that's wrong with this country, I can still say, "God Bless America." There is no other place on the face of the earth I'd rather be…in spite of how I got here. I'm not leaving and I don't see anybody else packing either…although we have the freedom to do so. I do not believe that it is the lack of opportunity that's destroying black America…I think its anger. Peace!

16

SITUATION: CRITICAL

Sitting down to write today is a bit like preparing for this past Sunday's sermon. I was ready to preach…and I felt like preaching but because of the message I had to deliver, I was not eager to stand up and deliver. Let me say first that barely a month goes by that someone does not request, or hint that I address certain issues in my editorial. I usually do not grant the request, or take the hint because I believe people should be bold enough to speak for themselves. Nevertheless, today is different. I'm going to write about the concerns of someone, including myself, whom I believe have a genuine concern for the youth of America, especially, our black youths.

Let me also say that as a Christian who's striving to be Christ-like, I cannot favor one race of people over another. Most of the Christians that I know and talk with do not feel the same but that's their problem. Being both Christian and lover of humanity, I have an obligation to address issues that seems to primarily affect a particular race of people and today that's exactly what I'm going to do.

Our black youths are dropping out of school at an alarming rate and we (African Americans) are doing very little, if anything, to stop this epidemic. We are simply ignoring, rather than addressing the issue. I hear all the time about how our young black men are going to prison but I don't hear anybody talking about "why" they are going. If I didn't know better, I would think that they are being rounded up because they are black and carted off to prison. There is a reason why so many of our young black men are going to prison and our young black ladies are getting pregnant…and I personally do not believe that it has a lot to do with discrimination, prejudice or racism. I think it has to do primarily with the lack parental training and supervision. Sure, it's better if a child has both parents in the home and both parents have a genuine concern for the welfare of that child. But it is indeed possible for a child to be successful having only one parent in the home. It's not easy…but it's possible. Because black people have persevered against incredible odds, I am convinced that we can achieve whatever goal we set for ourselves.

Graduating from high school is nothing when compared to what we're capable of achieving. There are certain standards that every student, regardless of race, creed or color, must meet if he or she is to graduate high school. If they do not meet those standards, then they are NOT going to graduate. We must understand and accept that those standards are not going to be lowered, nor should they be, to accommodate black people. We are not an inferior race and therefore, have the ability to learn as any other people.

We must stop listening to those in leadership in the black community who make excuses for our young black men and women dropping out of school. Most important, we must stop sending our children to school with the expectation that the teacher is going to do for them what we should be doing at home. Parents must teach their own children to be successful. Far too many black parents have become more concerned about how their child's hair look, rather than what's inside their head. We have become more concerned about the brand of sneakers they wear…rather than where they're going in life.

I'm telling you that if our young men do not stay in school and graduate, chances are that they are going to prison. If our daughters are not trained at home to be respectable young ladies, by respectable mothers, chances are they are going to end up pregnant and on some form of welfare. There are those who insist on blaming the high dropout rate among African Americans on racism and discrimination. But I'm telling you that, that salt has lost its flavor and is no longer good for anything except to be stomped out of the minds of those who insist on blaming the failure of our youth today on yesterday's injustice. Besides being black and deceased, what do Booker T. Washington (1856-1915), George Washington Carver (1860-1943), Fredrick Douglas (1817-1895), Thurgood Marshall (1908-1993), Mary McLeod Bethune (1875-1955), and Ida B. Wells (1862-1931) all have in common?

These icons of American Black History were all able to rise above the clouds of racism, hatred, prejudice, discrimination, etc., and become noted, outstanding, productive members of society. This was during a time in American history when trying to be like white folks, by getting an education, could get one whipped, run out of town, and/or killed. There is very little comparison between the acts of racism of yesterday and that of today. However, because of yesterday's atrocities, many of our African American youths are being fed with a spoon of discouragement, as racism, hatred, discrimination, and other forms of evil are being shoved down their throats.

I'm convinced that discrimination, prejudice, racism and hatred will always be a part of America but I do not believe that these evils are divided solely along racial lines. There are black people, white people, Hispanics, Indians, etc. that hate and discriminate against their own race... based on social status, last names, religion, body size, hair color and different points of view. There is just no end to these evil acts against humanity. If we are to have productive children, then we must start teaching them early in life to acknowledge God and treat others the way they want to be treated. We must also teach our children that if they really want something in life they must work hard to get it because no one is going to give them anything. We must also teach them that although our ancestors were brought to this country in chains as slaves...nobody owes them anything. Most important, we must teach them that getting what they want by illegal means is not an option...if he or she is to become a productive member of this society.

As a people, African Americans must understand that we cannot successfully move forward while looking back. History cannot be forgotten... but it can be forgiven. I've listened to many successful African Americans as they make excuses for our young black males dropping out of school. I'm always tempted to ask, "What's your excuse for being successful? How did you make it? Why aren't you teaching these young men how you overcame racism, hatred, prejudice and discrimination? Why are you instilling all this negativity into the minds of these confused young black men? Why aren't you telling them that once they get past being mistreated by white people that they are going to have to deal with being mistreated by black people? Why can't you really care for these young black men and women the way you say you do?"

I realized years ago that the so-called black leaders, black people saviors, don't really give a flip about our young black men because if they did, they would be addressing the "black-on-black" crime that's wreaking havoc on the black community such as robbery, assault, murder. They would address the fact that black people are feeding each other poison (drugs) that's taking fathers out of the homes and causing our baby girls to have babies. Not only does this successful black dude (black savior) not care about the young black men he's teaching to hate white folks, at the end of the day he's going to a home where drug dealers, prostitutes and other criminals are not quite so visible. He will only emerge from his safe haven again when there's another cry of racism. Remove the accusation of racism and discrimination and you'll pull his teeth...and cut his paycheck because he's a mere parasite that feasts off cries of racism and discrimination. For example, none of the black leaders are knocking on the door of the Governor's Mansion and asking why he has declared war on Crystal Meth but not crack cocaine, which has been wreaking havoc on the black communities of Georgia for the past 25 or so years. The truth of the matter is our nation's black leaders do not care any more for the welfare of black people...than white people and I'll tell you why.

A few years ago, three young black men was killed on the same night, in the same small Georgia town and no one marched in the street demanding that law enforcement do something about the violence and drugs that's destroying the black community. There were no appearances by any of our nation's prominent black leaders; nor did I hear of any concern expressed by any of the nation's black special interest groups (or organizations). On the other hand, a young black man gets locked up (not killed, or beaten) hundreds of miles away in Louisiana for fighting...and thousands march on that city demanding justice. In the mean time, back home the dope man is having a field day spreading his poison throughout the black community. He works the black neighborhood at will while everybody is off marching to teach white folks a lesson for locking up one of our young black men. But these three young black men gets executed in our own back yard and we don't say a word about justice...and we certainly do not demand it. Believe it or not, the ones accused and convicted of this slaughter, we will soon forget the reason why they were convicted and locked up. Instead, we will find a way to excuse their crime and focus solely on the fact that they are young black men in prison. What are we missing here?

I often wonder if I'm the only one to see what's really going on in the African-American community, or am I just the only one willing to say anything about it. I realize that it's not popular to tell the truth, especially when it comes to the speaking the truth about the black community but if we are to truly overcome, then we must know the truth before the healing can begin. However, if you're not black, regardless of what you see or think, you better keep your mouth closed and your thoughts to yourself, or you will be labeled a racist. It's a bit like black-on-black crime. We can kill, maim and degrade one another…but we dare anyone else to try it. On the other hand, if you are a successful African American with something to lose, you too better watch your mouth, or you'll end up in a meat grinder, or be accused of "trying to be white." Bill Cosby told the truth and was grinded to bits by some influential black people. Presidential candidate Obama hinted at what African Americans should be doing for themselves but then quickly backed off when he realized he was headed for the same grinder as Mr. Cosby.

I am African American and I have no problem admitting that we are NOT taking full advantage of the opportunities our ancestors suffered and died that we might have. Sadly, we seem to be saying to our forefathers,

"You have suffered and died for nothing…because we simply do not want to be successful. We are not going to take the time to see that our children do their homework; and we are not going to any teacher conferences to see how our children are behaving in school either. In fact, when they turn 16, they can quit school if they so desire but while they're in school, they might not know as much as the next child…but they're going to be dressed just as well as the next kid. Our kids can't learn that Algebra, Political Science, Geography and all that hard stuff being taught today. Shucks, we barely got school ourselves and that was years ago. Rather than hire a tutor, we have decided to buy our sons X-Box's, Play Stations, and expensive sneakers. As for our daughters, we'll just get her a cell phone with Unlimited

Text Messaging, or maybe an iPod, or maybe both. They can have whatever they want...except our time."

It's hard to believe that parents neglect their child in such a manner but it's happening every day. Nevertheless, no sooner than our young black men go to prison, because we did not spend the time training them "at home" to be successful, law-abiding, productive members of society... we start blaming teachers, law enforcement, white people and everybody else we can think of for their delinquency. The truth of the matter is, as parents we are not taking ownership of our children and therefore, not shaping their future. We must stop blaming...and start training. Racism, discrimination, prejudice, etc., have become punch drunk from taking so many blows. These evils exist in American but they no longer have the strength to hold us back. There will always be white people who believe black people are inferior and therefore, should be back in African (although, I've never been), or doing some form of labor that requires brawn rather than brains.

On the other hand, there will always be black people who will forever hate white people because of slavery and will never stop using this atrocity as an excuse for the lack of success in the African American community. There will always be those who blame everything that's wrong in the black community on white people, slavery, racism and discrimination...as if we are incapable of assuming personal responsibility. I listen to all this rhetoric and think to myself, "If we, as a people, are so weak that we cannot assume personal responsibility for ourselves by now, then we might as well have remained in slavery. If we're willing to give white people all this power over us, then maybe slavery should be legal." But I give black people more credit than that!

I do not believe that racism, or discrimination is strong enough to hold us back if we really want to move forward. It might not be easy…but it's possible. I believe this based on the great cloud of witnesses that includes Booker T. Washing, George Washington Carver, Ida B. Wells, Mary McLeod Bethune and Thurgood Marshall. These African Americans, as well as countless other successful African Americans Past and present), serve as proof that we are capable of staying in school, getting an education and becoming productive members of society.

It has long been my prayer that God choose Atkinson County, Ga. to serve as a role model for other counties, cities, states and nations to follow. Like other surrounding counties and cities, we are in desperate need of healing. I believe that this healing must begin with one individual, one family, one community, and one city at a time, which means that each of us must take individual responsibility for our own behavior, as well as that of our children. I do not necessarily believe that it takes a community to raise a child because if this is true, then it means that our children are doomed. The average black community in America is poverty stricken, infested with drugs, and drug- related crimes. I believe it takes a caring parent (two if possible) to raise a child. After all, God commanded parents to train their children…not the community. Our children might have to live in the ghetto for a while but they do not have to have a ghetto mind, if the parents will take ownership and teach them individual choice and individual responsibility.

We must teach our children that racism, discrimination, prejudice, etc., is the work of Satan and that his wicked devices reach far beyond white people mistreating black people. Let us not be so prejudice as to not teach them that in the beginning Adam and Eve "chose" to disobey God. They knew full well that they were wrong. Had there been blacks, whites, Hispanics, Indians, etc., in the garden, I'm sure they would have blamed another race for being evicted from Garden. The "blame game" has been around forever but it all comes down to individual choice.

Our sons participate in baseball, football and/or basketball throughout their high school years and when their running days are over, they turn to the streets because they only excelled in Physical Education. We then blame their delinquency on this great white conspiracy orchestrated to hold black people back. Now, I realize that this is football country and what I'm about to say is not popular, nevertheless, I must say it. It's no secret that many of our young black males are great athletes and excels when it comes to basketball and football. This does not mean that they are not capable of excelling academically; however, what it does mean is too many of those young males place more emphasis on the field and/or court than the classroom. When their classmates, the ones whose parents never let them forget the reason why they're in school, go on to further their education and become these young black men's employers, then it's perceived as a great white conspiracy. Put simply, black parents must decide what's more important, the education of their sons…or their sons' ability to play sports.

Every time I see a black kid catch a pass, make a touchdown, or shoot a basket, I wonder how he's doing academically. If it's your son, then you ought to have the same concern. Admiring a championship trophy, receiving a championship ring, reading about the game in the paper, or watching the game on TV won't feed him, put a roof over his head, or keep him warm in winter when his playing days are over…and they *will* be over. A "padded" diploma will not enable him to properly fill out an application and he's got to go to work somewhere, doing something, or he will end up in prison. I'm not against high school sports and I'm not saying that black athletes who don't make it to the pros make bad citizens but what I am saying is, parents should teach their children early that their future is more important than a high school championship. I think African-Americans should have the same rights as anyone else to play sports but for many, this right has become blinders that prevent them (and their parents) from seeing the purpose of school.

I've heard several reasons as to why so many of our young black males are dropping out of school. The reasons given depend on whom you ask. If you ask someone who still harbors hatred in their heart because of slavery, beatings, lynching and other miscarriages of justice perpetrated against black people by white people, then the fault is shifted far away from parental guidance and individual responsibility. There are those who keep their finger on the racism trigger, ready and eager to blame the high dropout rate among African American males on the lack of attention given them in the classroom. I don't really know how they justify it but they have narrowed it down to black males who have white female teachers…but I'm not going to insult black people, or anyone else by dignifying the reason with a response;

however, I will say that it's nothing more than stereotypical nonsense associated with the black man's sexuality.

I'm deeply troubled by some the successful African Americans whose hearts are hearts are filled with anger, hatred and vengeance. Rather than promote parental guidance and individual responsibility, many are making excuses for the lack of success in the black community. It's obviously different now than during the days when many black males had no other recourse but to quit school and help support the family. Parents, mostly mothers, had to choose between survival (food, clothes, shelter, etc.) and their sons' education. The father either did not make enough money to support the family, or had abandoned the family altogether. There were also many black fathers who remained in the home but supported more than one family…because of infidelity.

The lack of individual responsibility among African American males is a vicious cycle that's been spiraling out of control for generations now. If we continue to make excuses, rather than seek solutions, our young black males will continue dropping out of school…and into the penal system of American. We can place the blame on whomever, or whatever we choose but the truth of the matter is, the dropout rate in the state of Georgia is among the highest in the nation. I don't have the statistics on hand but I'm relatively sure that the dropout rate among African-Americans ranks the highest…when compared to other races in America. However, I am optimistic and therefore believe that once the idea of restitution for slavery has been put to rest, individual responsibility will become a reality. More of our young black men and women will get an education and become productive, law-abiding members of society. I have to believe that!

There are far too many young African American men and women today who seem to think that because of slavery we have paid our dues and therefore, have already earned our piece of the American pie. I believe this to be the reason for so many of our young black males continuing to defiantly sell drugs, in spite of having gone to prison. These young men are the product of what's been erroneously sown into their mentality. There were many successful African Americans today whose ancestors were slaves but once freed became landowners, homeowners, and business owners...only to have everything taken away or destroyed by white men, either by force or manipulation. Nevertheless, these African-Americans were determined to succeed and therefore, refused to allow past evils to hinder their present and future success. They had the option of either using their anger to fuel their advancement, or as an excuse to give up.

The type of anger and retribution I'm witnessing in the black community hurts primarily the people living there. Our young men are not standing in front of the banks, supermarkets, retail stores, hardware stores, and feed stores of American selling drugs. Even during riots, it's the black community that's destroyed. There is anger in the black community and there should be...but we have only ourselves to blame. As for retribution, it's merely an excuse to not work for what one wants. How can anyone explain retaliating against another race of people...by selling drugs and committing black-on-black crimes that wreaks havoc primarily on his own race?

Before the healing process can begin in the African American community, black leaders must first swallow their pride and admit that WE have a problem that only WE…with the help of God…can fix. We must put an end to the "blame game" and take a chance by teaching our children personal responsibility. Then will see our homes, community, city, county, state, and nation take a turn for the better. I believe that it will.

17

LET'S SAVE THE CHILDREN

A few weeks ago, I received a call from a young black lady who was undecided as to whether or not she should continue living with her mother, or move into her own apartment. She gave two reasons for her indecisiveness. First, there was the curfew. She had to be home by midnight. My response was, "As long as you're in her house…you have to obey her rules." The other reason she wanted to move out really surprised me because I know her mother. She told me her mother wanted her to "dump" her two female friends because they were white. She further stated that she had been told that she would never be anything more than just a nigga to them. She tried to explain to me how her friends "color" did not matter, and how she had difficulty relating to her own race. Before she could further explain her disposition, I interrupted by assuring her that her mother's views were stereotypical, prejudice, and wrong. The reason

I was so surprised by her mother's alleged statement is she claims to be a Christian.

It angered me that this racism was being fed to a child by a Christian. I realize that for many adults (of all races), it's too late to change their racist, stereotypical views…without the help of God…but there's still time to save the children. Although I never necessarily agreed with the bussing of children from one section of town to attend school several miles in another section, school integration provided all children with an opportunity to judge other children by the content of their character…rather than by the color of their skin. Our children deserve the opportunity to judge for themselves without mother or father's stereotypical views. We know that there's good and bad in everyone, in every race, and in every society. I talk with Christians (of different races) who often admit that they have to pray about "certain things" but some seem not to be praying sincerely because God is not prejudice. The truth of the matter is it's hard to pray for change…when you really don't want to it.

Our Children will learn whatever we teach them. If we teach them that a certain race of people is bad, they'll grow up believing such ignorance until they learn better. I can honestly say that whenever I hear my child talking about her school friends, she never refers to race…and that's a good thing. I'm much more concerned about their friends' character, than I am the color of their skin…thanks to Dr. King. History can neither be changed or denied; therefore, I believe where we're going is more important than where we've been. While it is important that our black children know their history, we should not teach them to hate or dislike people because of the past; however, only by acknowledging our past can we accurately assess the present and predict the future.

In conclusion, I see a movement in Atkinson County, Georgia, and America that cannot be stopped. Only the people can tear down the walls of racism, bigotry, and ignorance that have divided our county, state, and nation for so centuries. The government can enact laws but only the people can bring about change. Not everybody is happy about this change in race relations but it cannot be denied. Our children are the future of our county, state, and nation therefore, let us do our part to save them from the mistakes that we all have made in the past. I do not believe that anyone is born a racist. I believe that racism is taught, so let's stop teaching it…and save the children.

18

I HAVE AWAKENED

NOTE: The following is a speech written by the author and delivered at the MLK Day Celebration on January19, 2014 at Ebenezer Missionary Baptist Church.

"I don't know where I got the notion to take on such a huge task tonight but it's something that I must do. I thought it would be both beneficial and necessary to go back some 50 years to see what has been achieved since Dr. King's unforgettable, "I Have A Dream Speech." In his speech, Dr. King dreamed of a nation that would be kinder to African Americans, also known as Negroes back in 1963.

As I thought on these things, I imagined Dr. King standing here this evening…having awakened from a deep sleep, sharing with the congregation portions of a dream that is now a reality. I believe he would have entitled this speech, "I Have Awakened." I believe he would speak on this wise.

Harvey Williams Jr.

Back in 1963 I had a dream. I dreamed that one day this nation would rise up and acknowledge that all men are created equal. Well, that was some 50 years ago but today I have awakened…and this is what I see.

I see a nation in which laws have been passed that declares every man equal, regardless of the color of his skin. Not only that but all Americans now have a basic God-given right to be alive, to be free, and to be happy. I understand that a man's behavior cannot be legislated…and I understand that legislation cannot make a man my brother…but legislation can restrain a man from killing me, and that's good enough for me because I too have a right to live…the same as any other man!

I understand that legislation cannot guarantee that I will receive justice and I understand that legislation does not guarantee that I will not be wrongly convicted…but legislation can restrain a man from locking me up for trying to vote, or trying to sit on a certain bus seat, or trying to drink water from a certain fountain and that's good enough.

I understand that legislation cannot guarantee me happiness and I understand that legislation cannot remove bitterness from the hearts of men whose forefathers were slaves… but today legislation can restrain a man from denying me an education…or equal pay for equal labor…or the right to live in the community of my choosing.

I had a dream 50 years ago that one day in the most southern region of America, the ancestors of former slaves… and the ancestors of former slave owners…would be able to fellowship together in love, peace, and harmony. Today, I have awakened…and this is what I see.

Down there in South Georgia, somewhere in Atkinson County there is a small town called Willacoochee. Well, every

5th Sunday they have what's called the 5th Sunday Community Fellowship Service where black men, white men, black women, white women and little black and white children gathering in one place to worship Almighty God together. They are not concerned about race…and they're not concerned about religious denomination, as they lift up one voice…to one God. And I want you to know that after they have worshiped and praised the Creator, the one that made us all equal, they sit down together at the table of fellowship and they break bread together. Yes, I Have Awakened…and this is what I see!"

I also dreamed that one day the state known for lynching black men would become a state overflowing with black legislators and justice for all. Well, today I have awakened… and this is what I see.

In the year 2009, the state of Mississippi had 50 African American state legislators…being second only to the state of Georgia. Some of those same black men and black women who were oppress 50 years ago in the state of Mississippi…now sit in high places and are now able to assure that freedom and justice rain down on all the people…regardless of their race, creed or color.

I dreamed 50 years ago that one day black people would live in a nation where they would not be evaluated skin color… but by their behavior. Well, I have awakened…and this is what I see.

In 2008, Barack Obama became the first African American to serve as president of the United States of America; and in 2012, he was re-elected to serve a second term. Not only that…but in 2014, I witnessed Bettye Drayton-Williams make history, as she became the first African American to serve as mayor in the small southern town, Pearson, Georgia. That's not all I see since I have awoken but I'm going to stop right there.

Now in my closing…this is the least of what I have to say. I never dreamed that one day Almighty God would move upon this nation, touching the hearts of men to declare my birthday a legal holiday. I never dreamed that the day would come when the streets, avenues, boulevards, and parkways would bare my name. I never dreamed that a statue, chiseled out of the mountains of this nation, would be erected, bearing the image of a man who stood up and announced to the world that, "We Shall Overcome." I never dreamed that the government would shut down in recognition of this ole Atlanta Baptist preacher who gave up his life…that my brothers and my sisters would one day be free.

Now that I have awakened my brothers and sisters…I have a vision. I can see that we have come a long way. I can see that we have made lots of progress…but we still have a way to go. I can see the day when all God's children will be able to reap the benefits of the Promised Land. I see a day when all God's children will be able to join hands and sing in the words of the old Negro Spiritual, "We Are Free At Last!"

19

TO WAVE OR NOT TO WAVE

When I'm driving, my biggest challenge is not staying on my side of the road or driving the speed limit. No, the biggest challenge is deciding whether or not to greet the approaching motorist with a wave. I must admit that sometimes my decision turns into a game of "Chicken," as I wait until the last possible second before waving. There are also times when at the last second, the person I'm approaching will wave first and there's no time for me to wave back. When that happens, I throw up my hand, keeping it extended, in hopes that he or she will see me waving in their rear-view mirror.

Sometimes I just prop my elbow on the center console and simply extend my fingers when approaching a vehicle. This method does not always work because most motorist tend not see my fingers (or they know sincere greeting when they see it). I usually try to identify a potential greeter by his or her appearance but I'm seldom right. There are those whom I meet that I just know are not going to wave...but then they do. Those are the drivers that I hope catches a glimpse of me waving back in their rear-view mirror. Then there are the motorists that look friendly but will sometimes turn their head when I wave. There are also those motorists that you have to watch very closely because they will only extend a finger (or two) with hand never leaving the steering wheel. Finally, there are those like myself who play Chicken and will attempt to return my "last second" wave...forcing me to catch a glimpse of them in my rear-view mirror.

I must admit that when it comes to waving at motorists, I'm a little prejudice...well, maybe a lot prejudice. If I am approaching a black driver, I will usually wave without hesitation because the wave return ratio is usually somewhere around 95 percent; however, if the approaching driver is of Hispanic descent, I almost never wave for two reasons. One, the wave return ratio is usually very poor, meaning chances are he or she will not wave back. I also assume that most Hispanics do not understand my language and therefore, might not understand my wave either. I'll admit that this doesn't make any sense to me either...but it's the truth. If an approaching driver is a white male and I don't know him, I usually always wait for him to wave first because he may or may not wave back; and I don't want to send the message that I'm trying to be accepted by him. I'm just more at ease if he makes the first move and if he does, I'll gladly return the gesture. If the driver is a white female, I almost never wave first because I think chances are she's not going to wave back. Assuming that I'm right, I don't want to send the message that I'm interested in anything other than greeting (because of the way black males have been stereotyped) but if she waves I always wave back.

Now, that I've unloaded three years of "wave or not to wave," let me say this in conclusion. My decision to wave, or not to wave has absolutely nothing to do with dislike or hatred; instead, it has to do with "feelings." The true of the matter is, I'm hurt whenever I meet someone on the road and they don't wave…whether I wave or not. Assuming that there are others out there who feel the same as I do, when it comes to deciding whether or not to wave…I'll just wave and be done with it!

20

NEIGHBORHOOD WATCH

Last week, I watched as thousands marched on a small southern town in Louisiana, demanding the release of a young black man who's alleged to have been wrongfully incarcerated. I don't know the details surrounding the civil unrest but I do know that it is another race issue that occasionally spring up in America. Among the protestors demanding justice were several high-profile African American leaders, as well as college and elementary school students. I was reminded of the Civil Rights Movement of the 60's as I watched those demanding justice carrying signs and chanting, "No Justice, No Peace!" Unlike some protests in the past, this one ended peacefully with no acts of reported violence. However, several of the local businesses did close in anticipation of riotous behavior, instigated by outsiders but there was none. I was proud of the fact that African Americans demonstrated to the world that we are indeed civil and capable of dealing with any situation, including injustice, with decency and order.

As I watched the scores of mainly black people boarding the buses that would take them to the small southern town, I couldn't help but wonder who would watch the neighborhood while they were away. There was this allegation of grave injustice done to a young black man so many miles away but back in the neighborhood, crack cocaine and other drugs are destroying the livelihood of thousands of black people and their families...but no one is M.A.D. (Marching Against Drugs). I'm also concerned about the incarceration of the young black man in Louisiana, and someone should be addressing the act of racism (if that's what it is) but I'm also very concerned about the people whose lives and livelihood is being destroyed by drugs in the black community.

Both business and church heating and cooling units are being ripped from the foundations, as crack addicts remove and sell the copper contents to get high. Some addicts are becoming so desperate that they are literally dying to get high. It's reported that some have been electrocuted while attempting to remove copper from a power sub-station. Many of our young black men are dropping out of school and selling drugs in our neighborhood, to our people, and *no one* is addressing this problem...not even America's prominent black leaders. I would like to see some of these high profile black leaders take a more active role in addressing the problems associated with crack cocaine (and other drugs) in the black community. Georgia's governor has declared war on Meth but nothing is being done a bout the crack epidemic that continues to wreak havoc on the black community. I personally know of no African American that's addicted to Crystal Meth. Could this be another cleverly disguised form of racism? It seems as though many of our black leaders cannot see the forest for the trees.

The city of Adel, Ga. has organized a "Say No To Drug March" but this march will not draw national attention, nor will any of the nation's high profile black leaders be there. Selling drugs in the black community is black-on-black crime and no one seems to really care. We continue to convey the message that it's all right for us to destroy ourselves but we dare anyone else to mess with us.

21

WORK ETHIC

Work ethic begins in the home. It is my sincere belief that a child can actually graduate from high school and/or college with a 4.0 grade point average (GPA) and fail miserably in life...if he or she lacks good work ethics. Success involves more than studying and "acing the test." In fact, I believe one can be successful graduating from high school with a "C" average...if one's work ethics (attitude, feeling and belief about work) are good.

I think when an infant starts to walk, he or she ought to be trained not to leave their bottle and/or pacifier on the floor; instead, the child should be trained to leave these necessities on a table, or hand them back to the parent when finished. This can be done as soon as the child starts to tug on that soiled diaper...in an attempt to remove it. Kids will typically learn what we teach them...depending on when we start teaching. At the age of 5, I learned to pick cotton in Coffee County, Georgia. I didn't see any of the money I earned from the 30 or 40 pounds I picked but it taught me that one had to work for a living. When my brother and I were 6 and 7 years old, we moved to Willacoochee, Ga. and lived in the projects with relatives. We were assigned chores both inside and outside the apartment and the adults never gave it a second thought as to whether or not we would do what we were told. We were trained to be reliable…or else!

When we moved to the "West End" of town, we were sometimes without electricity, which meant wood had to be gathered out of the woods. My brother and I learned to find "lighter" wood that would light (ignite) the wood that would provide heat for cooking, as well as heat during the winter months. We could not afford a wheelbarrow so we carried the wood in our arms…kind of like carrying a baby. We were also at times without running water, which meant my brother and I had to bring water (daily) from three or four houses down the dirt road to our house. Sometimes we used a "foot tub" and/or a "wash tub" to transport water… depending on whether the water was to be used for washing clothes, dishes, or our bodies. We were approximately 9 and 10 years old at the time. Running water was a single spigot in the front yard.

While our mother worked for $2 or $3 a day, my brother and I were responsible for cleaning the house, raking the yards, washing and drying clothes (using a wringer washer and clothesline) and ironing. We were also responsible for feeding and supervising the other children. Being the eldest of the five children, I was in charge of the daily operation of the home when my mother was working. I cannot recall one occasion when I was discipline for failing to carry out my duties…not one. I took great joy in being temporary "supervisor" because it enhanced my self-esteem, self-confidence, and self-control (if I didn't like my assignment, I did it anyhow…without complaining).

When I was 12, I left my brothers and sister to live with my aunt and uncle in the country…on a farm. I was the only child in the household but I quickly learned to draw water from the well, cook, mow grass, and sew (hem pants). I also worked in the fields picking cotton, cropping/picking tobacco, hoeing corn, and pulling weeds out of peanuts. I find it strange that this type of employment is classified today (by some) as "slave labor." But back then, it was a means by which I could buy my own clothes and shoes for the upcoming school term, as well as have money to buy snacks and toys. I had a privileged childhood…although I had to work for what I got.

I forgot to mention that between the ages of 9 and 10, my brother and I were very skilled at cleaning fish, using a sharp knife but was never cut during the process. We even knew how to "dress out" the raccoons and squirrels that occasionally wandered too close to the house of a neighbor that owned a .22 rifle. Back on the farm, I was trained to cook meals, which included "cutting up" a chicken, baking corn bread, cooking peas, corn, okra, rice, etc. I took great joy in learning how to cook. During the hot summer months, when school was out, I worked the fields doing whatever labor necessary to make money to help with the operation of the household and to buy clothes for the upcoming school term. I did not want to dress the same as my classmates therefore, I ordered the majority of my clothes from a catalogue and they were not cheap. To afford these unique clothes, I worked in the fields.

Under the scorching sun, I pulled weed from rows of peanuts that seem to stretch a mile. I hoed corn, often feeling like I would suffocate due to the lack of air circulating among the tall stalks. I even picked a little cotton on the farm, sometimes walking bent over, or sometimes crawling from one end of the row to the other. I "topped" and suckered tobacco, which means I walked down the rows breaking the tops (blooms I used to call them) from the top of the tobacco and removing those little sticky plants from between the tobacco leaf and the stalk. I also walked behind the tobacco harvester and picked up leafs of tobacco that the "croppers" had dropped.

When I was 13 or 14 years old, I was promoted and given the most prestigious job I'd ever had…driving the Farmall tractor that pulled the tobacco harvester and/or trailer. The croppers would "strip" the tobacco on foot while I drove along side or just ahead of them. Every now and then, for amusement (I guess), someone would throw and hit me with a piece of tobacco stalk. I would start crying, stop the tractor, go to the boss and refuse to drive until he addressed the issue. Only then I would get back on the Farmall and finish out the day. It was a thrill for me to drive the trailed filled with tobacco from the field and onto the highway, down to the barn (or old abandoned house) where the "stringer" would be waiting.

The year after I was promoted to driver, I pulled a more sophisticated tobacco harvester…complete with a "baler" and two "handlers" on board. Every now and then I would lose my concentration (or nod off) and one of the croppers would yell, "RIGHT!" or "LEFT!" They weren't always nice about it because I'm sure they envied me. Not long after I started pulling the new harvester, I was "demoted" to cropper and developed a love/hate relationship with both the sun and the rain. The heat from the midday day sun was stifling and the tobacco leafs striking my face and bare arms became "tarry" and sticky. I would pray for rain to cool things off but when the rain came the problem went from hot to cold. The cold wet tobacco leafs drenching my body would cause me to shiver uncontrollably and I would pray for the hot scorching sun to reappear. I started to view this type of labor as cruel… but usual and necessary… if I was going to have the type of clothes (and other things) I wanted. Quitting was not an option, as working had become an acceptable way and a vital part of my life.

My last two or three years of school, I moved back to town with my mother, stepfather and siblings. Although I had left the farm, I continued to work the fields during the school break. When school resumed, I worked at the local sawmill during the evening to earn money for school meals and extra clothes. I was really proud of the fact that I had a means of making my own money. I didn't earn much but it was enough because I knew how to live within my means. I learned how to stretch one paycheck to the next because I didn't like being broke and stealing was not an option. My parents and guardians taught me that I had to work for what I got and that nobody was going to give me anything. Not only that, but I had witnessed the "welfare people" coming to my mother's house, going inside and "inspecting" to see if a man was living there and if we qualified for the government cheese and canned "meat" we received each month. I resented the invasion of privacy and vowed to never depend on anybody (or agency) for handouts because I did not like the humiliation, the lack of respect that came with receiving "free" stuff from the government.

The day after receiving my high school diploma in 1970, my work ethics (attitude regarding work) took a sudden turn for the worst. Two days after being hired at a trailer plant, I walked off the job and I would repeat this pattern 25 or 30 times over the next 17 years, even though I had a family to support. Working in the fields during the summer and at the saw mill after the school day was one thing but to be stuck doing strenuous manual labor for my livelihood was a different story; therefore, I had jobs that sometimes lasted two hours, two days, two months, and two years before I would walk away…for one reason or another. Being unwilling to work for a living, I found ways to supplement my income, which were sometimes both unethical and illegal.

I had convinced myself that the world owed me something…I guess for being born…and that employers were unwilling to pay me what I felt I deserved. I would work really hard during the first few hours, weeks, or months of employment but then I might talk with an employee that had been on the jobs for years and become discouraged; or I might suddenly realize the harder I worked, the harder I was expected to work and I didn't like feeling like a machine. However, I eventually found a line of work that I liked that did not involve manual labor, or require me to wear a uniform (always hated uniforms). This employment would last for six years…until I was fired. After being fired (forced to resign) over something really petty and denied unemployment benefits, I was right back where I started… unwilling to do strenuous manual labor for a week's pay.

My choice to make money "by any means necessary" resulted in the loss of my family and a relentless addiction to crack cocaine. Nevertheless, while addicted to crack, I realized that if my livelihood were to change for the better, I would have to go back to school or learn a trade. I chose the latter. I took a training class by day, worked part-time at night, smoked crack after work (when I had money), and would be back in class the next day. After finishing the training class, I was hired do manual labor but it was not strenuous. Although I was still addicted to crack, I really liked my job but it would not last. I returned to Georgia after only three months on the job and once again I was faced with having to do strenuous labor but this time my work ethics (attitude regarding work) had changed… drastically.

I knew my attitude regarding strenuous manual labor would have to change if I was to remain a free man in Georgia. In the city, I had sold drugs but I knew such behavior in my small hometown would be like volunteering to become a prison inmate; therefore, my only other option was to get a job like most of the other law-abiding citizen in the county. Besides, I had gotten sick and tired of trying to "beat the system" by searching for shortcuts to prosperity. Prior to leaving Florida, I had worked approximately three months as a security technician trainee after finishing a 3-month training class funded by the government. The class had prepared me for on-the- job training to install, trouble shoot, and repair security systems/telephones. I really enjoyed the line of work but should have taken the training more seriously because my trainer was not very patient…or pleasant. Being trained by a guy who thought I should already know certain things, coupled with my crack addiction, had started to threaten the good work ethics I was trying to develop. But I had grown tired of running away from my responsibilities and I wanted to change; therefore, I accepted the fact that I had to work for a living.

When I finally made the decision to return home, I knew what my options were regarding employment…but it didn't matter. I knew that I would not be working as a security alarm/phone technician because the nearest such employment was 18 miles away and I did not have adequate transportation; therefore, I prepared myself both mentally and emotionally to do strenuous manual labor…and strenuous manual labor I did. My first job (when I returned home) was picking up pecans and I, without hesitation, accepted. At age 34, I was now defeated and exhausted from 15 years of walking off jobs and trying get something for nothing. I was now crawling on hands and knees, searching for a pound of brown nuts…camouflaged among the brown autumn leaves that fell from the trees. At the end of the day, I suffered from sore aching muscles I never knew I had but I continued working…trying to better myself.

I picked up pecans, raked yards, unloaded 50 lb. bags of livestock feed (from semi trailers), as well as repaired and installed tractor and semi truck/trailer tires. I also braved the elements, working outside in the cold and the rain at 18 miles away. I also worked at a boat factory on the west end of town but was fired after being on the job three weeks because I could not "catch on" fast enough…and after damaging more than one expensive boats. I walked away sad and crying but I did not give up. I tried to find farm work (considered slave labor by some) but could not due to the time of year.

After six months of crawling on hands and knees, unloading 50-pound bags of livestock feed by hand, struggle to repair heavy semi/tractor tires, shivering in the cold and rain, and getting fired from jobs I really wanted to keep…I was hired by a giant retailer. I remained employed there for almost 12 years, five of which I was employed as a supervision. Because of my personal work experience, I can now tell others that if you (regardless of race or color) are willing to crawl on hands and knees to make an honest living, God will touch somebody's heart who will come along and extend a hand to help you to your feet…but you must be willing to crawl before you walk.

22

WE NEED TO HAVE A FUNERAL

A few weeks ago, a funeral was held in Detroit, Michigan with hundreds of participants marched behind the horse-drawn carriage carrying a simple pine casket adorned with fake black roses. People from every state came to show their "disrespect," including government officials, students, members of the clergy, and civil rights leaders. As the choir sang and the band played on the banks of the Detroit River, the eulogist prepared to deliver words of "discomfort." During this eulogy, nothing good was said about the deceased. In fact, everyone present thought death should have come much sooner. No one was sad or mourned, as the deceased was laid to rest at Detroit cemetery.

This was not your typical funeral. It was a mocked funeral, organized by the NAACP to symbolically bury the word, "nigger." Needless to say, the word though buried, was resurrected before the casket touched the bottom of the vault. Nigger is very much alive and well in our mouth, on the streets, in our homes, workplace… and even in our churches. The people I've witnessed using this demeaning word are primarily African Americans who either think it's hip or funny but I don't think it's either. Some of our black preachers and pastors use the term as freely as some of the Hip Hop artists.

If I was not African American and wrote the word "nigger" or "nigga" in an editorial, I would be labeled a racist and a boycott of the newspaper would be organized, regardless of how I use it. People across the nation would descend upon our small county, demanding both an apology from me, the paper and of course, my resignation. The message we convey to the world is that it is okay if we demean ourselves, we just don't want anyone else doing it. Somewhere between Africa and America, black women were stripped of their tiaras and labeled "Hoes." I don't think the white radio shock jock that referred to black female basketball players as, "Nappy Head Hoes" should have done so but we, black people, are credited for creating the word, "Hoe."

It's been said that certain racial slurs are not demeaning when spoken by African Americans. I wonder how long before we start referring to one another as Coon, Spade, Jungle Bunny, Crow, Spook, Sambo, Darkie, Gorilla, Tar Baby, etc. Right now, it's okay for us to be called dawg (dog) and boo (Jigaboo). Although I have removed the words "nigger" and "nigga" from my vocabulary (except when addressing the issue), I must admit that it has not been easy. I had to start "practicing" not using those terms, like I had to practice not using certain profanity when I became a Christian. Now whenever the word "nigga" manages to slip out of my mouth, I feel the same condemnation as when other profanity slips out. That's the way it should feel because it's a dirty and demeaning word...regardless as to who uses it. The church is the one place where black people should be able to go and feel like royalty. I don't think it's funny when someone refers to the congregation as "niggas," and the pastor as the "head nigga."

In conclusion, the mock funeral held in Detroit was a good gesture but this funeral must take place in the heart, mind, and psyche of the black people who apparently believe they are indeed niggas. I try to avoid the places where people refer to one another as nigga but when it invades the church, I have no other recourse but to stand and defend one of the only small pieces of decent ground left. We definitely need to have a funeral but the only way nigger is going to stay buried is it first has to die...but I don't think black people will ever allow that to happen.

23

CHECKS NOT ACCEPTED

A few months ago, I went into a local establishment to purchase items for the annual MLK Day Celebration. Standing in front of me at the register was an elderly white man who, when given his total, had the cashier fill out his personal check to pay for his goods. When I was given the amount for my goods and took out my checkbook, the cashier politely stated, "Sir, we don't take checks." I replied, "What you mean you don't take checks? I just saw you accept a check from the man that just left." The cashier replied, "I'm sorry, Sir. We just do what we're told." Seeing this person was between a rock and a hard place, I was not going to make his job any more difficult. The fact that the check of a white man was accepted, and mine rejected did not cause me to view it as a black and white issue, or a case of discrimination, or an act of racism. Instead, I chose to view the matter as a "Who you know and who knows you" issue. I didn't take it personal.

Although I had never written this place of business a worthless check, I completely understood their policy regarding checks. No establishment, in their right (business) mind, is going to turn down money; therefore, what I concluded was that the owner had been burnt one too many times by worthless checks. One of the employees behind the counter knew me and I could feel his distress, as he struggled to explain his position…without speaking negatively about his employer. I assured him that I understood as I reached into my pocket for cash to pay for my items.

I'm sure some of you are "seeing red" about now and you very well might have handled things differently but I really try to choose my battles…because some are just not worth fighting. I know we talk about not having respect of persons, treating everybody the same, the same rule applying to everybody, and all that good Christian stuff… but the truth of the matter is, we're all hypocrites in a sense because we *do* show favoritism; we *do not* treat everyone the same (we can't, because not everyone is the same); and we certainly *do not* enforce or apply our "personal" rules upon others equally.

I'm sure I could have contacted the owner of the business (who knows me) and my check would have been accepted but chances are, there would have been someone standing behind me, and the cycle would just start all over again. I chose to understand because I've been in several businesses where personal checks were taped to the counter, stamped with "NSF" by the bank for all to see. Most of those checks were written for items that were not of necessity because nobody "needs" $100 worth of seafood.

I could have chosen to write about this in a negative manner but I'm not a negative person and besides, this was "business" and not personal. The cashiers were neither black or white…they were employees doing their job. Some of you, I'm sure have reached the conclusion that I was discriminated against because I'm black but if that was the case, why did the owner of that business donate goods to celebrate a black man's holiday? I guess I'm saying that many times, discrimination, racism, and prejudice is in the eye of the beholder. Sometimes we simply "choose" to see only what we want to see.

I did not walk away that day angry…a little embarrassed…but not angry. In fact, I have since returned the place of business and made other purchases. However, my recommendation to the business owner is that he (or she) posts a "Do Not Accept Checks" sign so customers will know their policy before reaching the counter. By the way, I think displaying worthless checks in businesses is sleazy and very unprofessional.

24

PEOPLE PROBLEM

"We do not have a race problem in Willacoochee, Ga., Atkinson County, the state of Georgia, the United States of America, or the world. We have a People Problem."

Again, I present to you a comment I posted on Facebook last week. Social media provides me the opportunity to express my view of people, places, and things. Occasionally, I jump-start a strong debate. But for the most part, it provides a platform for me to express what I'm thinking…and how I feel about what I'm thinking.

When I posted the above last week, I was thinking how we have become addicted to blaming other people for everything that's wrong with the world today. We seem to have this misconception that if there were only one race of people on the face of the earth that the world would be a much better place to live. I personally do not believe the world will be the idea place to live until we all gone. I believe this because I think all human beings have "character defects," which is a decent way of saying that we're all messed up to some degree; and where there are character defects...there will be people problems.

As I write this, the country (if not the world) is awaiting the outcome of the grand jury's decision to indict a white police officer that shot and killed an unarmed black man. I don't know what happened the day the young man was gunned down but the thing that bothers me is, nobody seems to care about what caused this deadly encounter. People are fixated on "black and white" and nothing else really matters. No "defenseless" unarmed person should be shot down in the streets but I can tell you that the problem in the black community did not begin with this white man killing a black man...nor will it end there. When the dust settles in this tragic event, there will be even more killing of black men in the black community...and it will not be white officers doing all the killing.

The well-to-do white man who pulled the "Ponzi" scheme, bilking many white people out of their life savings, did not care that they were white...so long as their money was green. Nevertheless, we have this notion that certain races of people look out for their own and that very well might be true...if there's another race to prey on. When a kid decides to go into a school and shoot everything that moves, he does not see race. All he sees is people. The guy that detonated the bomb in Oklahoma City did not care about the race or skin color of the men, women, and children that perished in the blast. He views them as collateral damage... necessary to inflict a blow on the federal government.

There are even problems among "religious" people, whether the religion is Christianity, Muslims, and whatever else people choose to believe. I personally know Christians who do not like other Christians. Although these people are of the same denomination, the same race, read from the same Bible, attends the same church, and pray to the same God…they do not get along. (They really can't stand one another).

The one thing that most people in America, regardless of race, have in common is they tend to blame everything that's wrong with America on politics. People actually believe that their political party can make America a better place to live but I don't see political parties…I see people. I do not believe Republicans are smarter than Democrats, or vice versa… because they're all people and human beings have character defects. No. I'm not going to blame the world's problem on race because it's very obvious to me that the problem with the world is not race…it's people.

25

I'm Concerned

The following speech was written and delivered by the author at the 2006 MLK Community Service in Pearson, Georgia.

I'm concerned that our [black] history is not being taught in the classrooms of America…but I'm also concerned that many of our children are refusing to learn the history that IS being taught in the classroom.

I'm concerned about the lack of respect our children have for the law and those in authority…but I'm also concerned about the parents who are not teaching these children discipline in the home.

I'm concerned about the racism and discrimination that's still prevalent in our great nation…but I'm also concerned that we're not taking full advantage of the opportunities that we do have.

I'm concerned about those who still have the potential to lynch us because of the color of our skin...but I'm also concerned that bullets and knives are killing far more of our young black men than ropes ever have. I'm concerned.

I'm concerned about the drugs that flow through our community like a river and into the body and mind of our children...but I'm also concerned about how we tolerate this cancer and continue to blame others for the failure of our young men and women.

I'm concerned about our young men who choose to sell drugs rather than pursue an education...but I'm also concerned about the parents who allow theses young men to remain under their roof.

I'm concerned about the number of our young men that's going to prison...but I'm also concerned about the crimes these young men commit in our community. I'm concerned.

I'm concerned about our daughters who are so bold as to wear suggestive slogans such as "Bootylicious" across their backside...as if to say to the world, "This is all that I have to offer society."

I'm concerned about our babies having babies...but I'm also concerned about the parents who seem to take delight in raising little "Hoochie Mamas." Yes, I'm concerned.

I'm concerned about our young men and young women that are not attending our churches...but I'm also concerned about church leaders who are not setting a good Christian example for those who are attending church.

I'm concerned about those in high places that still tell nigger jokes...but I'm also concerned about those who have no problem being called "nigga" by their own race. Could it be that we have been programmed to believe that we are indeed, niggers?

I'm concerned about white Christians who still call black people, "nigger." But I'm also concerned about black Christians who still call white people, "cracker."

Last but not least, I'm concerned about the lack of unity among all Christians in America…but I'm also concerned about the lack of unity in the black Christian communities. Yes, tonight I am very concerned.

26

HIDING IN PLAIN SIGHT

Within five days of the Boston Marathon bombings, one suspect was killed and the other wounded and captured. Now, what that does that say to Americans and the rest of the world? If you commit a crime in this country, chances are that you will be tracked down and arrested…or worse. The latter is usually left up to the offender.

I used to be so naïve as to think that to elude the police, all I had to do was run and hide when I saw or heard that they were coming. What I didn't realize at the time was that the police were in my presence at the time…I just didn't know it. Some of my "customers" that hung out with me every day on the corner were the police. Some of my "employees" were also the police. These people did not have the authority to arrest me but they were talking to the people who did. It was only by the prayers of the righteous and the Grace of God that I was never arrested for selling drugs. A detective once came to my home (in Florida) and informed me that he knew what I did on the corner…but that he was not there for that. He there to inquire about a stolen gold necklace one of my "customers (and sometimes employee) had stolen from his teacher's classroom. The police turned up the heat on him and he turned me up. So, what am I saying?

When it comes to committing crimes such as robbery, thief, bootlegging, selling street drugs, etc., the police are hiding in plain sight. It could be the homeless guy or it could be the responsible guy that works a nine to five…you just never know; therefore, the best way to avoid jail and prison is to just do what is right. I think many of our young men are blinded by the fact that some alleged wrongdoers are never arrested and sent to prison. If this is true, I can tell you from experience that it's not because they're so smart as to avoid detection or capture…nor is it by coincident. One thing I have learned about human beings is…they love to talk. They love to tell what they know about who's doing what and besides, secrets are almost impossible to keep. Mix that in with a paid informant, or someone threatened with prison time, and these "policemen" hiding in plain sight will give up their Mama. Our young men need to understand that there really is no honor among thieves, especially when it comes to self-preservation.

I believe that God's hand is against those who perpetrate evil acts upon humanity, even though He allows it. This became my mindset when I made a decision to stop selling drugs. I came to believe that law enforcement would be victorious at least 90 percent of the time…because God is with them. As for the death and apprehension of the suspected Boston Marathon bombers, some might give credit to the video surveillance but cameras do not talk… people talk. Somebody had to put a name to the faces of these young men. It is my understanding that even before these terrorists struck, somebody had already informed homeland security that at least one of the bombers were a potential threat. The point I'm trying to make is there's very little that goes on in this country (and abroad) that law enforcement doesn't have knowledge of. Every now and then a criminal might manage to avoid detection but most of the time, the police are right there among us…hiding in plain sight.

27

CONSIDER YOUR WAYS NOW

I wasted several years using and selling drugs, trying to get ahead, only to fall back further in life. While I was busy trying to build my reputation as a drug dealer in South Florida, most of my classmates were making an honest living by working legitimate jobs. When I finally realized "Super Fly" and "The Mack" was only the figment of somebody's imagination, most of my classmates had a 16-year jump on me.

By the time I discovered the difference between Hollywood and the real world, I owned little more than the clothes on my back and I had no place to call my home. It was only by the Grace and mercy of God that during those years of trying to be "somebody" that I was not incarcerated or killed. Unfortunately, not everyone seeking notoriety will have the same testimony.

No long ago, Stanley "Tookie" Williams, a black man, was executed by the state of California for crimes he's alleged to have committed 25 years earlier. I don't know if he was guilty or not but he admitted to being co-founder of a notorious street gang with a reputation for violence. While awaiting execution on Death Row, Mr. Williams wrote several children's books, denouncing violent and gang activity but for him, it was too little, too late. The loved ones of the victims he's alleged to have killed were not impress by his change of heart, nor was the state of California. They both just wanted justice. The fact that this man had been affiliated with a street gang was etched into the minds of those seeking justice and therefore, probably outweighed any possibility of his innocence.

Karla Faye Tucker, a white woman, was executed by the state of Texas in 1998 for a murder she committed in 1983. While waiting on Death Row, she became a Christian and poster child for rehabilitated murderers but for her too…it was also too little, too late. Ms. Tucker, unlike Mr. Williams, admitted to the crime of which she was sentenced to death. Most of her supporters believed she was genuinely remorseful for the crime but it was not enough to bring back the person she's alleged to have murdered. The victim's husband never let us forget that this born-again Christian had buried a pick ax in the chest of his wife 15 years earlier.

Being in jail or prison is not the best place to consider your ways. Now is the time…while you're yet free to choose your meals, your clothes and what time the lights will go out. I receive letters all the time ending with, "It's about time for lights out." Every inmate with whom I correspond seems to have had a change of heart since being incarcerated. They tell me how God had to lock them down to get their attention; and most of these guys now know the Bible better than I. Nevertheless, having turned my own life around, I give them all the benefit of a doubt…until or unless they show me differently, which usually take only a week or so after their release. The point I'm trying to make is this. Most of these inmates seem to consider their ways and have a change of heart only "after" they have been sentenced to prison but it's best to consider your ways now…before you become a mere number.

As the day of execution drew near, Stanley "Tookie" Williams received lots of support from African American leaders seeking to save his life…but to no avail. During the 25 years he spent on California's Death Row, he had lots of time to "reflect and regret" but he could not go back in time and undo any of his (alleged) crimes. Unfortunately, the decisions he made as a youth cost him his freedom and his life. Karla Faye Tucker also received lots of support as her date with the executioner drew near. Many Christians and women supporters believed that she was a born again Christian and therefore, did not deserve to die for the gruesome crime she committed some 15 years earlier. Nevertheless, the state of Texas, and the victim's husband, would not forgive her past and she was put to death as scheduled.

I'm sure that many people have been incarcerated and executed for crimes they did not commit, simply because they were in the wrong place at the wrong time. Believe it or not, being with the wrong people can land you in the wrong place. My advice is to never place your life and/or freedom in the hands of the judicial system. Lady Justice is supposedly blind but sometimes she manages to peep underneath her blindfold and dispenses a different kind of justice, depending on who you are…or who you used to be.

"Tookie" Williams, like many of the young men in the black community, thought it was better to be known as a gang member (or thug), rather than not be known at all. Today, he's known internationally but he's also deceased. Ms. Tucker initially boasted about her crime because she, like many of the young black ladies in our community, was arrogant and had to prove that she was "tough as nails." She did prove her point but in doing so she also sealed her fate. What you do today can affect the rest of your life.

There is a well-known TV Judge that often talks about how, as a youth he joined a street gang and was eventually incarcerated. While incarcerated, he promised his dying mother, whom he says was deeply devoted to the church that he would turn his life around. However, when he kept his promise and attempted to become a productive member of society, his criminal past met him at The State Bar of Michigan. bar. Through perseverance and legal arguments, he eventually prevailed and became a lawyer, then a judge. In spite of his criminal behavior as a youth, he often reminds viewers that his mother insisted that he and his brothers attend church while in her care. I believe that it was this Godly training that contributed to his decision to change his life.

In my conclusion, I wish to encourage young men and women everywhere to take time out each week and attend a church of their choice. I am convinced, beyond a reasonable doubt, that had it not been for my Godly training as a child, I would not be sitting here today writing as a free man. I am pleading with every youth reading this to consider your ways now. Don't wait until you're sentenced to prison…or sitting on Death Row. I'm a living example that you don't have to go to prison to change your life. You can do it now…before the steel door slams shut behind you. Peace!

28

DADDY WAS WRONG

Not all prejudice people are prejudice by choice. Many were taught prejudice, hatred, and intolerance by daddy, grandpa and in some cases, mama and grandma. Because people they looked up to and admired taught them all these evils, their devotion to them will not allow them to change their perception of people of another race. I guess it's some kind of family pride but I call it foolish pride. Here's why.

I understand that daddy was a hard-working man who braved the elements (rain sleet, snow, and scorching sun) to clothe, feed and provide shelter for his family. I also understand that daddy actually invented a few things and did not steal or manipulate the copyrights from those who did not have the knowledge or money to have their invention patented. Daddy was an honest hardworking man...but daddy was wrong in many of his views regarding black and white men.

Daddy was wrong when he taught you that all black men were lazy brutes that only think about sex and want your women. He was also wrong when he told you that all white men desire to see you hanging from a tree. Daddy was wrong when he told you black people were created for the sole purpose of doing physical labor. He was also wrong when he told you that all white people wanted you back in slavery.

Daddy was wrong when he told you that all black people steal and could not be trusted. He was also wrong when he told you that white men would never give you an honest day's pay, for an honest day's work. He was wrong when he told you that black people were not intelligent. He was also wrong when he told you that all white men had a superiority complex. He was wrong when he told you that black people would take your jobs. He was also wrong when he told you that white men wouldn't hire you.

Daddy was wrong when he told you that God had cursed black people. He was also wrong when he told you that white people were blue-eyed devils. Daddy was wrong when he told you that black people were niggers. He was also wrong when he told you that white people were crackers. He was wrong when he told you that no white people were going to Heaven. He was also wrong when he told you that all black people are going to hell. Time has proven that daddy was just wrong!

I do not believe that a race of people exist that have not been taught something negative about another race. I believe God is saddened when He looks down upon the earth and see all the fussing, fighting and sometimes killing over who is superior…and who is not. It saddens me too! If daddy didn't teach you to love all people, regardless of race, creed, or color…and to judge people based on the content of their character, rather than the color of their skin, then daddy was wrong. It matters not that he split the atom or that he picked 500 lbs. of cotton in a single day. If he did not teach you that there is good and bad in everyone, in every race, then he was wrong!

By the way, I know daddy was a church going man and made sure his family also went every Sunday. He may have actually held an office in the church but I'm just curious about something. Did daddy ever say that he was a Christian?

29

SEEK PEACEFUL RESOLUTIONS

I'm huge fan of a female TV judge and whenever possible, I plan my weekdays around her show. I have nicknamed her, "Rude Jude," which needs no explanation. However, she is extremely sharp but seems always to be having a bad day. Nevertheless, she brings to the bench wisdom, fairness, complete control, and tolerates absolutely no nonsense. If she cannot control one or both litigants, she will promptly dismiss the case; moreover, she does not tolerate "sighs" or laugher from the audience. I've witness her on more than one occasion threaten to clear the courtroom if the court didn't, "BE QUIET!"

I'm going to share with you one particular episode of the show that inspired me to write this article. The case involved an altercation between an 8-year-old black girl and a 7 or 8-year-old black boy. The little boy had called the girl's mother "fat" and a fight then ensued between the two kids. Apparently, the little girl had help from another child, which resulted in the little boy getting the worst end of the deal. To get the full, complete, and true account of what "really" happened, the judge had the little boy take the witness stand to give his account of the incident. He stated that after his mother learned of the altercation, she immediately ordered him to get in the car and they both went to the house of the little boy that helped the little girl "jump" him. Once they spotted the child, the mother said to her son, "Now, go do what you gotta do!" The little boy stated that he reluctantly got out the car and proceeded to swing away at his little friend. Yes, the boys were actually friends.

Needless to say, the judge was furious as she proceeded to yell at the mother, telling her that she was an "IDIOT!" This mother was teaching her son to fight, rather than seek a peaceful solution. The judge then dismissed the child from the witness stand and proceeded with the case, which was actually about the altercation that occurred between the adults. After the little boy had finished doing what he "had to do" to his pal, the "take-nothing-off-nobody" mom proceeded to the house of the 8-year-old girl and confronted her, which resulted in a physical altercation with the little the girl's mother. During the fight, the aggressive mother lost a large patch of her hair that will never grow back. Now she was in court suing the little girl's mother because she lost her hair during the "Big Payback." She failed to realize that had it not been for her "unwillingness" to seek a peaceful resolution, she would not have been sentenced to a life of wearing weave…to cover the spot where her own hair once covered her scalp. Nevertheless, she proceeded to explain to the court why she felt she should be compensated for her lost. Although the judge allowed her to state her case, the expression on her face clearly conveyed, "Are you nuts? What's wrong with you?"

The saddest part of the entire episode was not the boy being commanded to fight his friend. It was sadder that the mother could not understand, or refuse to accept the fact that she was wrong in teaching her son to fight...rather than teaching him how to seek peaceful resolutions, as opposed to war. Chances are this kid will grow up and teach his children to do the same but hopefully, every time he looks at his mother's head it will serve as a reminder that it's better to seek peace resolutions rather than, "Doing What You Gotta Do." By the way, not only did the mother lose a patch of hair, she also lost her case because the judge "did what she had to do." She dismissed the case.

30

GRAVE DECISIONS

I do lots of boasting about my hometown Willacoochee, Ga. and people better not say anything bad about Atkinson County in my presence. As for as I'm concerned, New York and all those other big cities ain't got nothing on us but it wasn't always like that. Now before you jump to the conclusion, thinking this is another one of those "Somebody's Done Somebody Wrong" editorials…hear me out first.

I attended Atkinson County Training School, an all black institution for black students from 1966 to 1970. I'm not sure why it was called a "training" school but it produced some well-trained individuals who went on to make their mark on Atkinson County and the world. The year following graduation, the school system was integrated…in a way. It's my understanding that the school transportation system remained semi-segregated several years following integration. I'm told the students were separated by race and gender, i.e., black and white female students rode together on buses to and from school and black and white male students rode together on other buses.

Believe it or not, I just asked my daughter (20 minutes ago) if this was still happening and of course, she just laughed and said, "No, Dad." Now, I don't consider myself a black activist, so I really didn't know and I don't have the time, or the energy to go around looking for black and white issues. However, I do remember a time when, if you were a Negro (as blacks were known back then) you could not eat in the same facility as white people in Atkinson County. The local churches were also segregated back then. Now for you who might be thinking, "He need to leave that alone," I say this. It's good to recall where God has brought you from... so you can better appreciate the present and know where you need to be in the future, which brings me to my next point.

I was attending a Willacoochee City Hall meeting a few years ago, when the subject of the local black cemetery came up. There were a few concerns regarding the condition of some of the graves such as, broken slabs, no identification markers, trash, etc.; but the most important issue mentioned that evening was the fact that the black cemetery was rapidly reaching its capacity. It was suggested that we haul dirt in and expand the cemetery but then someone rejected that idea because of an underlying waterbed problem, or something (don't quote me on this). Then it was suggested that more land east of the graveyard be cleared to make more room for the deceased but then I think someone mentioned that someone else owned the land.

A year or so after the meeting at City Hall, I was interviewed by a The New York Times reporter. She asked me about race relations in Atkinson County and, Man, I couldn't wait to tell her how far we've come over the past 20 years or so. I was so excited to tell her how well black, white, and Hispanics were getting along in our small southern city. She nodded and smiled but in a very calm, serious toned asked, "How many cemeteries are there in Willacoochee?" Just as I started to wonder what her question had to do with race relations, I got one of those Edith Bunker's, "Oooooooohhh," moments. When I told her we had two cemeteries, she jotted something down on her pad and asked another question that had nothing to do with cemeteries.

Every since that interview, I've wondered what will happen when the black cemetery is full. Will we integrate in death, or will we remain segregated? One day, my brothers and sisters will have to make a Grave Decision.

31

I KNOW WHAT IT'S LIKE

Driving through the urban streets of Atlanta on yesterday, I noticed several images of hopelessness, sadness, brokenness and defeat, although it was Christmas…a season to be merry. What I witnessed was a clear reflection of the wretched man I was 25 years ago. As I was driving, I silently renewed my vows to God, promising that I would never forget to remember where whence He brought me.

I know what it's like to walk the mean streets of the city, not really knowing where you are going…but yet you're going. People riding by and looking at you in disgust because all they see is a homeless bum. They can't see the pain inside, nor can they see the man you were before the troubles of this life beat you down. I know what it's like to spend Christmas without your family and wondering what your kids are doing. Wondering if they are happy. Wondering if they miss you. Wondering if you will ever be reunited with them.

Wondering if you will ever experience another Wonderful Christmas. Believe me, I know what it's like.

I know what it's like to wake up each day, hoping it will be your last. You wish your life would end but lack the courage to end it. You walk the mean streets of the city at night without so much as a pocketknife because in a sense, you want to be a victim. If you ever see a man walking in the middle of a busy intersection, as though he's wants to be get run over…well, its because he probably does. I know what it's like to lie down at night with no hope for tomorrow. You wish that the night will never end, that it will last forever but you know that it will not; therefore, you hope that your dreams will take you to a place where there is no tomorrow…if only for an hour. I know what it's like to hold on when there is nothing to hold on to. You hope for the best but expect the worst. You walk around in a daze, as if in another world because in reality you really are. The world you were born into is much too painful; therefore, it's much easier to just get high and merely exist…rather than get sober and try to live. Yeah, I know what it's like.

I know what it's like to be in the company of many… but yet be alone, having no one to talk your troubles over with. Everybody around you is laughing and talking but deep within you know that, like yourself, everyone there is hurting, as they try to smoke their problems away. I know what it's like to have loved ones reaches out to you but because of pride, you refuse to extend your hand and receive their love. You prefer to beg, borrow and steal…rather than admit defeat. All your life you heard that Jesus is the one that can make it better but you're too proud to admit that what you heard might be true, although you know all your choices have been wrong.

I know what it's like to have people praying for you, although you can't see or hear them. You notice people all around you are falling but yet you stand…supported by a force that you cannot see. You know that it's not of your own power because you really just want to lie down and die. I respect the man living on the urban streets of Atlanta, Ga., as do I the man in the White House because I know what it's like…to be down and out.

32

PEACE OF MIND... PRICELESS

In the mid 60's, I looked forward to sitting in front of the black and white TV to watch Elvis Presley movies. This guy could sing and dance like no other white man I'd ever seen and like most other black kids my age, the color of his skin did not matter; nor did his ability to act. I have to admit that Elvis was my first idol. In 1970, the Jackson Five burst on the scene just as I was about to graduate from high school. Before I saw the group on TV, I was told that the lead singer was an eleven-year old kid named, Michael. Not only could he sing but could dance as well. I remember wanting to be like Mike.

While training to be an auto body repairman at Gary Job Corps Center (Texas), in 1971, I became an admirer of Huey Newton, co-founder of the Black Panther Party. I was attracted to the black clothing (especially the black beret) that the militant group was known for wearing. I was also attracted to the assault weapons, and raised clenched fist (salute) that signified Black Power. Being a young black man at the time with no sense of direction, I would have risked both my life and freedom to be like Huey. He was a man admired by millions, while I was nothing but an unknown corpsman. Then there was Marvin Gaye, internationally known for his ballads of love, peace, war, sex, divorce, God and the ecology. I became convinced that everything I needed for my soul could be found in his music. Although he did not profess to be a Christian (that I'm aware of) but yet he was blessed with all this earthly wisdom and godly talent. Not only did I listen to the words of his songs...I felt them as well. Marvin, in many ways, became my god.

During the latter 70's and early 80's, I started to covet the lavish lifestyle of the South Florida drug dealers. Most of the time, I was unemployed with little or no money and the local dealers were always flashing wads of cash. I drove an old Ford (when I wasn't walking), while the drug dealers drove flashy, customized cars. I wore common clothing, while the dealers seldom wore the same designer clothes twice. I had a wife and three children, while these unfaithful criminals had several women and several fatherless children. The man with the dope became my role model. When I saw the money, fame and power that these men possessed, I was filled with envy and I wanted to be like them. I learned years later that what looks good from a distant...close up ain't never that good!

Elvis is reported to have died in 1977 at age 42 from a drug overdose. Michael would spend millions in defense of allegations of child molestation. Last week, he died at age

50 (allegedly) from an overdose of a medication that should have been used in the operating room. As for Huey, he was shot to death in an alley during an alleged drug transaction that went awry in 1989. He was 47 years old. Marvin, shot and killed by his father in 1984, is alleged to have been a drug addict. He was killed one day shy of his 45th birthday. The South Florida drug dealers I once coveted either ended up in prison, dead, or became their own best customer. All the wardrobes, wealth, weapons, wisdom, and women were not enough to give them the peace of mind they so desperately craved. I thank God that I discovered in time that money, Fame, and power cannot give what mankind craves the most, peace of mind, which is priceless!

33

PIMPED

There's a young man whom I've known for most of his 27 years. God-fearing parents trained him and he was very active in the church, playing drums and singing in the choir. However, during his senior year in high school it became obvious that his behavior was taking a turn for the worst. He started dressing thuggish and hanging out with people known for their criminal behavior. Moreover, he became very disobedient and disrespectful towards his parents, which is usually the first step towards prison.

Seeing where this young man was headed, I pleaded with him to get a good education so he could get a good job. I also encouraged him to honor his parents so that he might have a long prosperous life. He respected me as I instructed him and always responded with a very polite, "Yes Sir." However, I could feel that my words were falling on deaf ears. Nevertheless, I had to at least try. Not long after he graduated, I receive word that he had started selling drugs, which was no surprise because "birds of a feather flock together." I knew that it was only a matter of time before he ended up in prison. But I still felt an obligation to warn him, so whenever I saw him I would encourage him to do the right thing. There was still the polite, "Yes Sir," only now it was adorned with a mischievous grin.

One day while leaving a restaurant, I saw this young man accompanied by several females drive by in an expensive car. He blew the horn and waved high, as he flashed his "Look at me" smile. Although he gave the impression that he was pimping, I knew from experience that he was the one being pimped (more on the subject next week). A few weeks later, I received word that he had been arrested on a very serious charge, including possessing and selling drugs. I also received word that he wasn't taking being incarcerated very well, which meant he was doing lots of crying (literally) and making those very expensive collect calls from jail to his parents, only now he's treating them with respect…as he begging them to get him out. When I heard he was locked up, I sent word to him that I would come and visit with him as soon as I could. I wish he had been truly listening when he replied, "Yes, Sir" to the advice I was giving him. Had he listened, he would not have been locked up (without bond) and facing 25 years to life. I found it necessary to forgive him for trying to destroy those whom I was trying to help stay away from drugs.

Although I hated the young man's criminal lifestyle, I've always loved him like a relative. Whenever my love for him started to fade, I would remember that I too was once blind and could not see the truth. Just like so many others in the black community, this young man sought a shortcut to having the finer things in life and as a result, he allowed himself to be pimped (more on that later). Hopefully, he will learn before it's too late that there are no short cuts in life. One either walks the "straight and narrow" or takes up resident with the crooked. I believe that he will one day sing in the choir and play the drums again. The question is, will he do so as a free man or an as prison inmate?

There seems to be a genuine concern among African Americans regarding the number of young black men being lost to the penal system. It's been reported that black males make up the vast majority of the prison population in America. The question is, why are so many of our young men being incarcerated? Are they being incarcerated because of the color of their skin? Are they being incarcerated because no one will hire them, giving them no other recourse but to engage in illegal activities? I've heard many reasons as to why so many of our young black men are going to prison and to be honest, most of what I hear does not make any sense. Maybe I'm just not smart enough to figure out the great white conspiracy aimed at incarcerating our young men. However, I do have a theory, based on my own personal experience, that makes a little more sense (to me).

Our young black men are simply allowing themselves to be pimped. Like prostitutes, many of our young males are being pimped by those who actually own the drugs that they (our young black men) sell primarily in the black communities of America. We are so consumed with identifying our enemies by race and color that we overlook the real enemy. The white man, although he supplies the drugs, is not the one distributing drugs in our community, destroying lives and livelihoods along the way. I think it's time that we start identifying our enemies by the content of their character...rather than by the color of their skin.

Our young men are being pimped by a system that's seemed designed to take them out of the community, away from their families, and rob them of their freedom. Maybe this is the great white conspiracy I've been hearing so much about. Nevertheless, the gleam of chrome wheels and gold/platinum teeth has blinded them so that they cannot see the 6 by 8 brick and steel cell awaiting them. They never stop to as why they are only allowed to sell drugs in the black community. One does not need a PhD in Common Sense to know that our young black men do not "own" any drugs. Many live with their girlfriends, who are on public assistant; or they live with their parents, mainly their mother. Our young black men simply do not have the resources to get drugs into the country. They are being pimped by those who have the resources (connections, planes, boats, etc.) and actually own the drugs.

American is one of the most intelligent countries in the world and very little happens here (of importance) that the government does not know about. One does not have to work for the CIA to know that a $300 vehicle with $3,000 wheels, parked at the housing projects...is not the product of a man working for a living. Our young men in the drug trade seem to be satisfied with their pay, which amounts to the crumbs that falls from the table of their pimp. Throw them a fancy ride, a little gold, a few dollars, a little recognition, one or two sack chasers (female that pursue drug dealers), and they're satisfied.

Many of our young black males that are still in school view the older prostitutes (drug dealers) in the community as heroes. Most of the dealers are uneducated but able to ride in a fancy vehicle, have lots of cash and jewelry; therefore, they don't see a need to stay in school. As a result, many will dropout began the migration into the penal system. Could it be that we are blaming the wrong people for the dropout rate among our young black men? We have been blaming the pimp when it's actually the prostitute.

As a young man living in south Florida, the thought of hustling for a living became very appealing to me in the mid 70's and early 80's. Like many of our young black men today, I became obsessed with many of the fictitious black characters I'd seen in the movies. Like many of our young men now imitate gangster characters on the big screen and in videos, I wanted to be Superfly (really ashamed to admit this but I must) and hustle on the streets, selling drugs for a living. I was too naïve at the time to distinguish the difference between fact and fiction. I lost my job in the early 80's and was angry and as a result, I convinced myself that selling drugs was a necessity, rather than a choice. I chose not to work for minimal wages and I risked my freedom to be a so-called hustler. On the streets, I was very careful as to whom I sold drugs to and I actually worked harder than if I'd had a legitimate job.

I would analyze every car that passed by the corner, trying to see if the occupants looked like cops. Can you believe that? Whenever I went up to a car to make a sell, my heart would be pounding like mad, as I used every ounce of my extra sensory perception (ESP) to determine whether or not I was selling to someone who actually wanted my product…or if I was a bout to sell to the police. After five or six months on the streets, I considered myself undetectable and untouchable, as I witnessed other street level pushers on the same corner get busted and carted off to jail. One evening while taking a break at home, there was a knock on the door. I looked through the peek hole and immediately recognized the middle aged white gentleman on the side. He was a know city detective. I didn't panic because at the time, I had far less than an ounce of marijuana in my possession but was waiting to re-up (purchase more).

When I opened the door, the detective asked, "Are you Harvey Williams?" I told him that I was and then said, "I know they call you "Slim" on the streets, I know what kind of car you drive, I know what you do for a living and as you can see, I know where you live; but I'm not here about that. I want to know about a stolen necklace you bought on the corner." I assured him that I had not bought a stolen necklace and he assured me that he knew I was lying. After a few minutes of exchanging accusations and denials, he turned to leave but left me with, "I'll be watching you."

It was true that a student had exchanged the stolen necklace with me for a bag of marijuana, but I wondered how the detective knew about the transaction. Moreover, I wanted to know how in the world he knew I was selling marijuana. Other than the fact that I was on the corner daily, wearing 25 or 30 gold and silver (mostly silver) necklaces and medallions, I appeared to be just another guy on the corner…in my mind. Within two or three days following that visit, I learned that there were students on the corner that were actually working with the police, taking mental snapshots of the events taking place on the corner. Some of these informers were actually good "customers" of mine. When I learned what was really going on, I realized that I was not so undetectable and untouchable after all; instead, I was just plain dumb. I wasn't avoiding jail because of my hustling skills, I was merely being "allowed" to sell marijuana on the streets. I then realized that I could be scooped up any time and hauled off to jail. But my pride would not allow me to stop hustling and get a legitimate job. I decided that I needed to work my way off the streets and became a dealer…selling to street level pushers.

Let me pause here and say, the essence of this article is to in no way meant to glamorize my criminal past; instead, it's intended to warn the young men who desire to hustle, rather than work for a living, that you are not nearly smart enough to outwit the law (the older dealers already know this), you are merely being allowed enough rope to hang yourself. Lynching is almost unheard of in 21st century America but many of our young black men continue to hang themselves. Although, the rope is being supplied, no one is forcing it around anyone's neck. They are doing it to themselves and eventually will swing from the tree.

We complain about how many of young black men are in prison but we say and do nothing when we know they're engaging in illicit behavior. Although drugs and violence in our community are destroying scores of our people, our nation's highest profile African American leaders remain silent but for the injustice of one black person, they lead thousands to march afar in protest. I'm looking forward to the day when our black leaders stop chasing cameras and become genuinely concerned about the people. It's been said that many of our young men have no other choice but to engage in unlawful and illegal behavior but I do not believe that. In fact, I know better. We live in a country where armed guards are posted at our borders to prevent illegal immigrants from entering into this Land of Opportunity. These men, women, and children are risking their lives (and even dying) to come here to do work that Americans refuse to do.

Recently, I heard a pastor say that many of our young black men resort to selling drugs because they cannot find meaningful employment. That's not an excuse! When I stopped engaging in illegal activities some 20 years ago and returned to Georgia, meaningful employment for me meant doing a honest day's work…for an honest day's pay. My first "meaningful" employment was picking up pecans. I crawled on hands and knees picking up pecans. I know for a fact that selling drugs in this neck of the woods of America is not a matter of survival…it's a matter of choice. The iron shackles of slavery have long disappeared but a new form of slavery has emerged. Many of our young black men have become enslaved to drug distribution, drug addiction, violence and other destructive behavior. When will we stop blaming outsiders for the problems that we obviously have within our community?

Racism in America is alive and well but in the black community, it is the distribution of drugs, drug addiction and other black-on-black crime that's destroying the livelihood of the people living there. We have a problem and unless we face it, we're going to lose a whole generation of our people…if we haven't already. So what can we do to rectify the problem? I believe the first step toward healing is to view the problem through unbiased eyes, looking beyond race or color and accepting the truth. Opportunities for African Americans are probably not going to get much better than they are now, so we'd better start taking advantage of what we already have. Staying in school and pursuing higher learning is probably the biggest opportunity that we have, and will ever get. I see much of our opportunity to advance being wasted, as many of our young black men are pursuing the gangster dream, rather than the American dream. Some blame the teachers, saying that the black male is so intimidating to white female teachers; therefore, he does not receive the same attention as others of another race.

I do not claim to know all the reasons why so many of our black males are dropping out of school…and into prison but until I can figure it out, I am going to suggest they stay in school and out of trouble. We must teach both our sons and daughters the importance of fearing (acknowledging and reverence) God, the value of getting an education, and then motivate them to become law-abiding citizens. We must then see that it happens and not leave it up to their pastor, teacher, or the police. Many of our children are rude and arrogant because they have not had proper behavioral training in the home.

Training children involves more than teaching them how to hold a fork and spoon, or use the bathroom. A child has to be taught values, starting at a very early age. They have to be trained to do that which is right because they are born knowing how to do wrong. It's true that many of our young black men are uneducated and unemployed. As a result, many cannot find employment that will allow them the privileged of owning the finer things in life; therefore, many resort to doing whatever's necessary to get the things they want and by doing so, they become easy prey for predators seeking to pimp them…by having them sell their drugs. If you're an uneducated, unemployed young black male, your chances of getting pimped are far greater than those who are educated and employed. One does not need an education, good credit, or clean urine to qualify to be pimped. Even one's criminal past is a plus.

There's lots of anger among the young black males in our communities because they are working long hours on the streets and having very little to show for their effort. Although he readily flashes his wad of cash, the majority of the $1, $5, $10, and $20 bills does not belong to him. At the end of the day, he must report to his pimp (who usually also has a pimp) and pay for the drugs "fronted" him (loaned to him on credit). With the few dollars left, he has to support his own habits (40-ounce malt liquor, marijuana, females, etc.) and make those high payments on the fancy ride/wheels, which he's managed to get financed at a very high interest rate…because his credit is bad. Unlike the master pimp, the one he never sees, he cannot appear as an ordinary guy. He cannot save, or put aside his illegal gotten gain so that he will have sufficient funds to pay for his defense when…not if…he's busted. He can't drive an ordinary vehicle because he's addicted to flashiness. He has to flaunt his stuff to boost his self-esteem. He openly risks his freedom to prove to himself and others that he is somebody. He tells those whom he call, Brothers how the "Man" is holding them back but in reality, he's the one holding them back. If you don't believe it, try not paying him for the drugs he "fronted" you until payday. He couldn't care less about you not having a place of your own to live, or that you need to feed your family, or keep a roof over their head. He just needs you to pay for your drugs…so he can pay for the drugs "fronted" him.

Our young men, like prostitutes, are being allowed to work the streets of our community and infect as many as are too weak to cope, or escape the clutches of addiction. Every so often, one a pusher is scooped up and taken down (probably to be squeezed for information concerning other maters) and released back into the community to wreak more havoc. However, when these menaces to society are incarcerated for any length of time, we're not satisfied until they're back on the streets, selling drugs in our community again. It matters not that they are contributing to the delinquency of our children. In our minds, if they're black it's all right. Those of us, who genuinely care about the people losing their lives and livelihoods to drugs, must make our voices heard. Just recently, I witnessed thousands (most African Americans) leave their community to march for the (alleged) wrongful incarceration of a young black man in Louisiana, yet nothing is being done to set free those bounded by black-on-black crime (drugs and violence) in their own community. I will say again that we seem to have been brainwashed into identifying our enemies by the color of their skin, rather than by the content of their character.

As a young man, I lost my footing as I threaded on forbidden ground for over 15 years. My mother trained me to be a God-fearing, productive member of society and I was taught the difference between right and wrong; nevertheless, when I reached the age of "do what I want," I chose to do wrong. I grew up in the midst of racial discrimination but I never heard my mother utter one negative word about any race of people. Therefore, I was not taught hatred as a child. Whenever I complained about the racism I experienced, she told me to pray.

I remember this white man from the finance company coming to the house one day and harassing my mother about money she didn't have. I was between 10 and 12-years old at the time and when he really started disrespecting her, I picked up a rake and was prepared to go to jail… or worse. But she told me, in a very calm voice, to put it down and I did. The man also calmed down and soon left. I never saw him again. I was trained to be nonviolent and I was also trained to work for what I wanted. When I started neglecting my Godly training after leaving home at age 19, I could not justifiably reach back into the pot of racism and pull out one single excuse for my behavior. I could have easily looked back on how the white man had disrespected my mother and used that as an excuse to rebel against society but I did not. However, I did rebel against society but had nothing to do with racism. It was because I had not prepared myself for life after high school. When I should have been learning, I was busy indulging in attention seeking behavior, like so many of our young black men today, who are more interested in touchdowns and baskets… than they are test scores. Is the coach, who's probably more concerned about championships than the welfare of our young men, to blame? Parents, who's looking out for the future of your sons?

As a youth, I experienced my share of racism but most of the maltreatment I endured came from the bullies of my own race. I was picked on, picked at, punched and made to cry because I was the eldest child and had no one to defend me. I never told my mother because she had enough problems of her own to deal with but on more than one occasion, I contemplated killing my assailants. Had it not been for my home training, I would have probably become a murderer. I grew up hating no one. When I tried to hate another race of people, I would remember how I was treated as a youth by my own race; therefore, if I were going to hate anyone, then I would have to hate them as well.

I liken the community drug dealers of today unto the school bullies of my youth, only they are worse. Whereas, I concealed my maltreatment from my mother, the mothers today are crying, as they witness their love ones being destroyed by the people who call them brother and sister. The mothers of those wreaking havoc on the black community are also crying…as they visit their loved ones in prison, accept their collect calls, or lower the lid of the coffin slowly, as they look upon the face of their sons for the last time

If we're going to help our young black men stay out of prison, then we have to tell them the truth and the truth is, no one can hold them back if they really want to succeed. Racism and discrimination in America might get better but it's not going away. I realized long ago that there will always be people that think they're superior to others but what really matters is, how I feel about myself…and I do not feel inferior to any man, regardless of his race, creed or color.

Having respect of persons would render me ineffective as a Christian; therefore, I must reach out to all men. However, it seems to be the African American male in this country that stands in the need of guidance more so than others. The question is, what are we going to do about it. Are we going to continue ignoring the problems in our community and looking at problems elsewhere…or are we going to start cleaning around our own front door first? Will we ever be able to convince our young male that by being "allowed" to distribute drugs in their own community…is a form of racism at its cruelest? They terrify their own people, mostly during the day while rays of the sun reflect off their custom painted vehicles and their high polished wheels. They do not wear white sheets to conceal their identity because their egos demand that they be known. They do not carry ropes, except the golden ones around their neck, but they won't hesitate to beat, maim or kill an "uppity" brother (or sister) who becomes a rival…or a brother or sister who can't pay on time. Does any of the above remind anyone of a dark period in our American history? We don't need the Klan to do to us what we're doing to ourselves.

Being a black man, I'm able to take an honest, unbiased look at what's really happening in the black community and what I see is drugs, and drug related crimes destroying far more of our young black men than that's ever swung from a tree for being uppity; or beaten, shot and killed for whistling at a white woman; or being falsely accused of rape, or trying to vote.

Fathers are still being snatched from their families and sold into slavery in the form of drug addiction by those being "pimped" by their masters. Our young innocent daughters are still being taken away to provide pleasure for those being pimped and in the process, becoming breeders for the next generation of slaves. Our mothers are still crying, as they witness their loved ones being carted off to jail, shot, maimed and killed by the community's task masters, who must keep the master's money flowing; or else they will suffer the same fate. When will our young black men stop being pimped by white men?

It's not that drugs are not being used in other communities; it's just that our young black men are not allowed to openly infect the people living outside the black community. In fact, they'd better not so much as be seen cruising certain neighborhoods, or else they will be pulled over and a "reason to search" will emerge…from somewhere. Our young black dope peddlers know the rules therefore; they seldom wander outside the confines of the black community. We are perishing for lack of knowledge. More attention is being given to the small blister (racism) than to the cancer that's eating away within (drug dealers). I can't remember the last time I heard our nation's high profile black leaders mention drugs. In fact, I've never heard them mention drugs at all, although drugs and drug related crimes remain the biggest destroyer of the African American male. However, should one of our black males be mistreated by a white man (or someone of another race), these high profile black leaders are the first on the scene, being second only to the media. Where there is no camera, chances are you will not find high profile national black leader. Are they being pimped too?

It's been said that black men get more time in prison than others who commit the same crime. I'm not disputing that but I will say, we might need to start avoiding behavior and activities that sends us to prison in the first place. If we know that the judicial system is unfair when deciding justice for our young black men, then we must find a way to convince our young black men to stay out of trouble and… stay in school. Black History should be a required subject in our school so those still angry about slavery can see that not very much has changed over the past 140 years…only the taskmaster. Many of our people are still chained and bound by drugs, and drug related crimes. Today's taskmasters are those who sell drugs and commit other black-on-black crimes in the black community. They supervise those that are chained and bounded, doing their best to prevent any from escaping. They report regularly to their white masters, who gives them a "Good Boy" pat on the head for every father taken out of the home; and for every son sent to prison; and for every daughter who becomes a single parent and forced to rely on public assistance.

Selling drugs and engaging in other illegal activities because "the man" is doing us wrong is nothing but an excuse and a desire to get rich quick. If our young black men are going to stop going to prison...then they must stop allowing themselves to pimped by the people sending them there.

34

THE BEAUTY OF GOD'S NATURE

The highlight of my day is to walk a lone country road, or wander off deep into the Georgia woods where no one knows I'm there except God and his creation. Sometimes during my evening stroll, I can't help but think about the possibility of meeting someone who might not be too happy about something I've written in an editorial. I also think about the possibility of a surprised encounter with a female bear that's determined to defend her cubs, even though I'm not a threat to them. There's also the possibility of stumbling upon a marijuana field, or Meth lab and the owner/operator…who might not be glad to see me. I tell myself that I'll probably exercise caution and stay off the country road and out of the woods but then nature calls (no pun intended) and within a day or so, I'm back at it again. I just can't resist the beauty of God's nature.

Along side the country road, I see a small shallow brook surrounded by trees. I stand there for several minutes being entertained by the birds diving from the branches and into the water. As I'm witnessing this unusual display of nature, I can't help but wonder why these lovely creatures are diving into the water. Then God reminds me that it's hot and that birds also take baths. It's then that I realized the purpose of birdbaths in the yard, and what I'm now witnessing is nature at it's finest…the way God intended it.

A little further down the road, there is a cow pasture in which I notice a mother cow and her new born calf. Judging from the afterbirth still clinging to the mother, had I been there a few hours earlier I would have witnessed a natural birth, complete without midwife or doctor. As I get closer, a few of the cows stop grazing when they see me approaching and within seconds, as if by some secret code, they're all now watching me. Out of the herd, a fearless bull appears and walks along side the fence, never once taking his eyes off me. Although, he has no horns…I'm glad the fence separates us.

A few yards away, perched on a fence pole is a majestic hawk. From a distant, I observe him through binoculars and the beauty of this creature of nature captivates me. As I move in to get a closer look, it flies away and perches high upon a nearby tree branch. I stand there for the next five to ten minutes watching him, as he watches me. He's apparently waiting for me to leave, as I'm waiting for him to come closer. Soon he loses patience and soars off into the woods, squalling, as if voicing disapproval of my invading his space. The next day or so…we do it all over again.

Not only have I timed my walk to dodge the heat of the day but to also get high on the setting sunset. Alcohol, tobacco, cocaine, marijuana, and crack (cocaine), has never done for me that which God's radiant orange/red sunset does. Whenever I want to get high, I just make a date with the setting sun. I know the exact time and place to be when I want to watch it disappear behind the silhouetted trees on the western horizon. With camera in hand, I capture the various degrees of its descent so that on those days when I can't witness this phenomenon live, I can watch it on the computer screen and take a mental flight back to that place and time. Oh, the beauty of God's nature!

As for the people whom I meet on this lone quiet country road, well, they all know me now and all are very friendly. At first, they would to stop and offer to help me, thinking I'd broken down. But when they see me now, they just smile and wave because they realize that I'm just out there walking and enjoying…the Beauty of God's Nature.

35

YOUNG BLACK MEN

To be completely honest, the mere title of this article makes me feel somewhat racist because as a human being, it is my sincere belief that I should not favor any one race over another...not even my own. As a Christian, my brothers and sisters in Christ should be closer to me than my biological family...if I understand the scriptures correctly. Anyway, the violent death of young black men in America is often overlooked, until one loses his life at the hand of someone who is not black. This is an issue that we are well aware of but are doing very little, if anything to address it.

Not many people I've talked with lately seem to think the death of a black man, at the hand of another black man, is as tragic as a black man gunned down by an overzealous neighborhood watchman; therefore, I can't help but wonder if we really care about young black men dying in the streets, or do we just like being a part of something big...such as media coverage. A few years ago, my young nephew was executed along side country road and it barely received media coverage…even though he was not the only young black man killed that night in that same county, regarding the same "incident." In fact, days after these murders occurred, I was told by law enforcement that these crimes would probably never be solved. I knew then that very little, if any effort would go into solving these murders…probably because they were drug related.

A few years prior to my young nephew being executed, there was another multiple homicide in the same county but nobody protested, nor did anyone demand any type of justice. It was as if black people were afraid to even mention these murders because the alleged killers were young black men. So, I can't help but wonder, do we really care about our young black men being slaughtered in the streets, so long as other young black men slaughter them? This seems to be the message we are sending to the world. I think the death of all young black men should receive lots of media attention because this is an epidemic in the black community that we seem to be ignoring.

I've heard people say that they are angry and feel sorry for the parents (that they only know through media coverage) of the high profiled slayings of young black men at the hands of non-blacks. But as for the parents next door, whose son is violently killed by another black man, these parents quickly become a fading memory. I just don't think the media should dictate how much value is placed on the life of a young black man…but until African Americans start valuing the lives of these young men, nobody else will.

It's been said that, other than war, young black men are the biggest killer of young black men and it certainly appears that way. I'm bothered every time I hear of any young black man being killed, especially, in a violent manner. I am concerned about the violent death of all victims and their families, regardless of their race, or color but it appears as if African Americans lead the pack when it comes to the slaughter of their own people. There are those who will argue that the media only reports the violence that happens in the black community. I don't really know what's happening in the north, east or west but in these small southern towns, I know there's a lot of black people killing black people. We blame a lot of this violence on poverty, fatherless homes, lack of education, etc., but I think we need to instill in our young black men the value of life and that black lives matters too.

36

WHAT WE DO KNOW

We may never know exactly what happened on August 9, 2014, the day a young black man was shot and killed by a white police officer in Ferguson, Mo. I'm not going to name the deceased because to do so would make his death appear more important than that of the other hundreds of young black men killed in this nation each year. However, we do know that this incident stands out because the young black man was *not* killed by another black man; and that he did not have a knife, gun, or anything "legally" classified as a weapon on his person when he was shot multiple times by a white police officer.

We do now that there was something about the young man's behavior that caught the attention of the officer. I think most witnesses that day agreed that the young man was walking in the streets, disrupting the flow of traffic, which was not only an act of defiance...but also illegal. So, we know that had this young man been obeying the law, the encounter between he and the officer would never have occurred. We do know that. Most witnesses, according to the media, will agree that there was a physical altercation between the young man and the officer, which means the young man was probably resisting arrest. In other words, for those who might not understand, the young man disrespected authority by disobeying the officer commands…whatever they were.

What happened next will depend on whom you ask. First report was this young play man was surrendering, with his hands above his head, when the white officer shot him down in the streets. It was later reported that the young man was charging the officer when the officer open fire and killed him. So, we may never know the truth as to what happened on that fateful day in August but we do know that a young man lost his life. We do know that following the death of this young black man there was looting and burning "in the neighborhood of the deceased" but nobody can give me a reasonable explanation as to why. I know the looting and destruction of property had nothing to do with the death of a young black man because if that were so, many of our cities today would not exist. I used to think this barbaric behavior was about revenge (never believed it was about the lack of justice) but it I was wrong. I have yet to hear reports of fires and looting in the white officer's neighborhood. We do know that most people don't care if you burn your own house down…so long as you don't touch theirs. We do know that.

We do know that the looting and fires in Ferguson has nothing to do with black people caring about the well being of black people. We know this because not even "black owned businesses" were spared during the mayhem. Nevertheless, there are educated, law-abiding, black productive members of society who actually justify the destructive behavior triggered by the young black man who refused to comply with the law enforcement. They argue that he was unarmed and defenseless but not having a gun, knife, baseball bat, etc., does not necessarily make one defenseless...especially, if you're good with your fist.

Except for family and friends, nobody seems to really care about the violent death of young black men in America. Young black men kill unarmed young black men (even unarmed innocent black women and children) every day in the black community and nobody strikes a match...except to grill. The evidence proves that a black man's death in America only becomes important (for the most part) when a white man kills him. We do know this...whether we admit it or not. Last week, while the fires were still smothering in Ferguson, Mo., another grand jury refused to indict police officers involved in the death of a black man resisting arrest in the state of New York. Again, there is widespread protest and minor scrimmages between demonstrators and law enforcement in various cities (thank God for Atkinson County) but so far, there has been no burning and looting as in Ferguson. Also, unlike the death of the young black man in Ferguson, Mo., the death of this black man in New York was captured on video, in which we clearly see him resisting arrest and eventually being taken to the ground in a choke hold. Again, I don't know why he and law enforcement crossed paths but it's my understanding that he was violating the law (doing or attempting to do something illegal). What I do know, according to the video, is the deceased resisted arrest and struggled with several members of law enforcement.

I'll be the first to admit that any person in position of surrender should be allowed to do so, even if they initially resisted, without receiving further harm or death. But we also need to understand (and teach out children) two very important aspects of life. First, if you violates/breaks the law, chances are you WILL have an encounter with law enforcement. It does not that a genius to know this. Second, if you resist arrest, you are very likely to be beaten, pepper sprayed, tased, and/or shot by law enforcement. We do know that officers are NOT going to say, "Well, we see he's having a bad day. He's resisting arrest, so let's just leave him alone." Nor will law enforcement say, "He's is black. If we arrest him, we might have a riot on our hand. So, let's just leave him alone."

Now we do know that none of the above is going to happen. So, if I do not want to be beaten, sprayed, tased, and/or shot, then I need to first, obey the law and if I'm so brazen as to break the law, then I subject "myself" to be beaten, sprayed, tased and/or shot. I do not need a PhD to understand, "Put your hands behind your back," or "Get down on the ground." There is nothing complicated about preparing oneself to be arrested. However, I'm almost to the point of believing that not everyone is capable of grasping what I'm saying here.

I think what we need, especially in the black community is for more law-abiding, black productive members of society to start teaching our people to first, obey the laws of the land; and second, how to stay alive if confronted by law enforcement. Instead, what we have is far too many law-abiding African Americans, productive members of society, justifying the unlawful behavior of those dying as a result of bad choices.

For every one person that's teaching black men how to stay alive, there seems to be 100 teaching them the opposite...and/or justifying why so many are not law-abiding, productive members of society. We all need to understand that if you should die while resisting arrest, people might remember your name, protest/riot in the streets, have T-Shirts printed, bearing your image, and your family might even profit from your death...but you will not. On the other hand, if you obey and comply with law enforcement, chances are you will live to fight (legally) another day. Having a grand jury render a "No Bill" verdict is much better (for you) if you are alive to hear it...than if you are dead and cannot. We all do know that...don't we?

37

RESISTING ARREST

"If I happen to be on my way to church, dressed in a white suit on a rainy Sunday morning and the police pulls me over and tells me to get out of my truck and lie face down in the mud...that's exactly what I'm going to do."

The above is an excerpt from a training session for young black men conducted at Willacoochee House of Deliverance Church a few days ago. Our young men need to understand that if law enforcement comes for them, chances are they (law enforcement) will not leave without them. It does not mean that the authorities are always right but they do have the right to come for you...and you have an obligation comply and accompany them. Resisting arrest, for any reason, will only make matters worse. It makes more sense for me to simply turn around, put my hands behind my back and allow myself to be handcuffed...rather than be pepper sprayed, tased, struck with a baton (or fist), bitten by a dog and/or shot…and then be handcuffed. This is the mindset I hope to instill in young men and women everywhere.

I was taking an evening stroll in the country one day when a state trooper noticed my truck parked on the side of the road. I watched as he backed up and sped to where I was now standing and waiting to show him my identification, plus answer any questions he might have. I was really annoyed because there's nothing like taking an innocent walk in the country but I was not going to display any signs of anger…nor was I going to reach for my id without him telling me to do so…because I was not going to be an accident.

He was not very kind as he demanded to know why I was "out here" walking and why I parked beside the road. Now, this was not a main highway. This was a country road named after of a local farmer. It was obvious to me that this man was testing me to see if I would put up any type of resistance. Although he was questioning me as if I was a child that had run away from home, I remained civil and responded with, "Yes, Sir" and "No, Sir." He may have been an officer of the law but he was a human being first and human beings have character defects and therefore, I was not going to give him a reason to pepper spray, tase or shoot me. It was just he and I on this lonely stretch road and no way was I was not going be around to tell my side of the story. That was my mindset at the time. No, I did not like the manner in which I was approached but his words did not hurt nearly as much as pepper spray, a baton or a bullet would have, so I just let him do his thang. However, the more respect I gave him, the more civil he became and after

5 or so minutes, he told me to be careful and drove off… without ever asking to see my id.

I could have gone into a "Why did you stop me?" mode but it wasn't really important…even though I had a right to ask. What was most important to me was the fact that I had stopped on a lone road by a man with weapons and the authority to use them (at his own discretion) and I needed the departure to be as smooth as possible. Had I really been concerned about why I was stopped, I would have contacted his superiors because the first thing I did when he drove up was look for a name or badge number.

There are people that apparently prefer to be tased, sprayed, beaten, and charged with resisting arrest, rather than surrender to law enforcement. It makes no sense to me but…To Each His Own. If I must go to jail, then I prefer to be in the best of health because being locked up is punishment enough. I'll leave you with this, "If they come to take you away…defend your rights another day."

38

HEALING

I have been writing about problems and healing in the black community since 2002 and to be quite honest, it's taking every ounce of hope left in me to remain the least bit optimistic. Since I don't when, it's been taboo for black people to address the issues plaguing the black community… without at least blaming other people for what's wrong. For that reason, not many black people are willing to step up to the plate and say what needs to happen, so that we might be healed. Those who find the courage to do so are often met with sharp criticism, as if black people have been picked out (of other races) for ridicule but sometimes it's hard to not look at what you see…and this is what I see.

I see far too many single parent households in the black community, usually mothers trying to raise one, two, three, or more children. I'm not so sure it takes a village to raise a child but it does take good stable parenting…if a child is to have any chance at success. We have too many parents that do not understand that training for success begins in the home. Too many of our children are given the latest sneakers, Smartphone, Xbox or PlayStation and not enough (if any) chores; therefore, they grow up with no sense of responsibility. Having no sense of responsibility, many seek to have the finer things in life without earning them, which often lead to encounters with law enforcement.

Too many "daddies" in the black community do not understand the importance of creating life. Like many species of the animal kingdom, they simply impregnate one female and move on to the next, leaving the responsibility of raising the child to the mother. Too many of these "daddies' care more about a fancy vehicle than they do the life they created…and far too many mothers allow them to do so. Many of the "daddies" that pay child support, pay no attention (to the child). As a result, daughters grow up looking for love in all the wrong places and sons grow up lacking a positive role model.

There is a serious lack of parental supervision in the black community. What I mean by parental supervision is, those who take the time to examine video games, movies, and music before purchasing it for the child. For example, most parents would not so much as entertain the thought of purchasing a porn DVD for their daughter…for obvious reasons. But when it comes to purchasing violent videos for their sons, they think nothing of it. They don't bother because they do not understand the impact that all the violence has on the psyche of the child. At an early age, these kids are introduced to extremely graphic violence (punching, stabbing, shooting, blood, guts and brains) but these parents think, "It's just a game." Needless to say, too many parents are failing to monitor their child's Smartphone, which often leads to teenage pregnancy (babies having babies), making it even more difficult for the mother to receive an education.

Parents are not monitoring their children's progress at school. We have far too many of our children operating a Smartphones…but cannot use a calculator. Parents seem more concerned about why their child was denied recess… rather than why their child received and "F" on his or her report card. They tend to take school as a form of daycare, rather than an institution for learning. As a result, black people lead the nation in illiteracy, and the dropout rate among black students is the highest in the nation. There are those who say the teacher is to blame but I blame the parents. The role of the teacher is (mainly) to educate…but it is the duty of the parent to motivate.

When accessing the problems that plague the black community, one must not fail to understand that we are talking about a people that have over 400 years of catching up to do. No number of programs will heal those years of oppression overnight but my message to the people is, "Don't give up…while trying to catch up." Black people began the journey of freedom just a little over 150 years ago with nothing. We owned nothing except maybe the rags that concealed our nakedness. We had no home, real estate, businesses, money, or education; nor could we speak the proper language. All we were given was religion and a Bible…to interpret the best we could.

When taking all those factors into consideration, one can understand not only why the black race comes in last when compared to other races in America, one can understand the anger of the black community as well. However, my message to the people is, if we are to overcome, we must not fight those who are in position to help us. Instead, we must lose the anger and start building meaningful relationships. We must find a way to look beyond slavery and see the sacrifice our ancestor (unwillingly) made that made it possible to live in a land flowing with milk and honey…the greatest nation on the face of the earth. We must strive to find our place in America because like sheep, we are lost and need a shepherd that we can see and touch (God created mankind to be helpers one to another). We cannot get where we need to go alone. We must learn from and follow those who know the way if we are to ever catch up…whether we like it or not.

Black parents must become better shepherds for their children. Left alone to find their proper place in America, our people will never catch up. A child, for the most part, only knows what he or she is taught, see, and/or hear. We must understand and accept the fact that raising a child is a J-O-B…and it's a very important job. Unlike livestock, they require much more than food, shelter, and a place to sleep at night. They have to be "trained" if they are to be successful. They cannot be winded up like a toy and sent off to school for a few hours and be expected to live meaningful lives. It's not going to happen.

I will be so bold as to say that not all individuals are created equally…but race has nothing to do with that. Our children are just as capable of learning as any other race but like any other race, they are not all capable of achieving the same thing…but they can achieve something. Not all will make the honor role but we won't know who's capable unless the parent gets involve in the child's education. In a sense, the parent has to go back to school…for the sake of the child. They must familiarize themselves with certain aspects of the child's education by learning "why" the child is not making the honor roll. The teacher can only lead children to the water but he or she cannot make them drink. If the child is to drink from the fountain of education, then it is the parent that must do the persuading. The teacher alone simply cannot do this.

Parents must become more concerned about their children's academic achievements, more so that their athletic abilities. But before I go there, I want to address what's not being taught in the classroom, or on the basketball court, the baseball field, or the football field. There are some things that can only be instill in a child by the parent, a guardian, or a mentor and without these things, our children will continue to come in last...in spite of academic and/or athletic achievement.

I believe the one thing that will take our children our children up the ladder to success the fastest is respect for others, starting with God. There was a time when black children had to attend church services, whether they wanted to or not. Before the Xboxes, Play Stations, Smartphones, etc., there was the parent. There was a time when our children were exposed to, what sometimes amounted to spiritual entertainment, at least twice a week. We were either part of the church service or we merely sat and observed. Either way, we had to be there. Children attending church in the black community today is more so a choice (their choice) than a requirement and as a result, many have no respect for God or anybody else. The community tree, the place where alcohol is sold and consumed, has become a hangout, or place of refuge on Sunday...rather than the local church.

Children do not respect their parents and parents seem helpless to do anything about it. Not because they fear being charged with child abuse but because they fear not meeting their children's approval. Daughters tell their mothers what they want to wear, which too often causes males to focus their body...rather than their brain. Sons demand (in a subtle way) the latest Xbox or PlayStation that's often saturated with violence, which results in them becoming desensitized to fighting, stabbing, and shooting people. Both sons and daughters become adults as soon as they receive a Smart Phone. Because of the parent's respect for their children's right to privacy, they do not monitor their children's phone, or how they communicate on social media. Children simply cannot be children when they are allowed to be adults.

Children today do not respect the elderly. There was a time in the black community when every adult was a parent to the children living in that community, which meant if a child was told to do something (or nor do something) by an adult, he or she obeyed. Try that now and you not only get cussed out by the child but also by the parent. If the village today is not raising children, it's no fault of the village. Blame the parents...the ones who are likely to cry foul when their child gets expelled from school.

Alternative School has been established (mainly) for students who have no respect for educators but before there was an alternative to attending regular school, there was Reformatory "Reform" School. Corporal Punishment is now considered cruel and unusual but there was a time when it was a method of teaching not only respect...but academics as well. It does not work today because most children do not receive any form of meaningful punishment at home, which is evident by the lack of respect shown for others. There was a time when both the teacher and the parent disciplined students who were disrespectful but if parent do not discipline their children, they are not going to allow anyone else to do so…except the police. Our young black men make up the vast majority of the prison population because they have no respect for the laws of the land. Those killed at the hand of law enforcement is primarily due to their lack of respect for law enforcement and other authority.

It makes no difference as to how fast they run, how many baskets they score, how many touchdowns they score, or how much they achieve academically. If our children are not taught to fear God, their parents, the elderly, educators, the laws of the land, and law enforcement, they are going nowhere fast…except to the prison and/or the grave. Peace!

39

WHERE DO WE GO FROM HERE?

How does one correct a wrong? How can those who have been mistreatedbe compensated? When is enough compensation enough? I am convinced that some questions simply have no answers. At least, not answers that will satisfy everbody. History paints a very vivid picture of the plight of black people in America, so we know full well where we have been. Where we are today will depend on who you ask. Some people cannot see past slavery and other atrocities perpertrated against black people whenever a black person dies at the hand of someone who is not black. So, if you ask those people where African Americans are today, they will tell you that we are no closer to achieving civil rights and justice than we were four hundred years ago.

Integration was thought to be a down payment towards compensating black people for wrongs suffered at the hands of white people. It was to be the cure for illiteracy, delinquency and poverty among black people living in America but with integration came the loss of what little "blackness" we had remaining. This new form of compensation gradually started erasing what little black heritage we had remaining. There was a rapid decline in black owned businesses and we became more "whitenized," as black educators decreased… and white educators increased. The government forced the integration of our physical being but could not intergrate our minds and souls. Any attempt at having a "Black America" was lost with the introduction of integration and therefore, we are still were not pleased. Some wrongs simply cannot be corrected.

As for education, we were now being taught by the same teachers as white students but somehow, we still became the minority when it came to graduating from high school… especially when it came to our young black males. Some accused white female teachers of neglecting these young black males because they feared giving them too much attention might be misinterpreted as meaning something more than trying to help them achieve a proper education. As a result, of these young black males became discouraged and simply dropped out of school…or could not score high enough on the SAT to enter college, which caused them to end up in prison. I think this is another excuse.

We seem much more concerned about our past than we are the present and the reason for that might be found in a quote by the philosopher, George Santayana: "Those who cannot remember the past are condemned to repeat it." This quote seeems much more acceptable, even among many black Christians, than the Apostle's Paul instruction to forget (let go) the past and move forward. The question is not where have we been, or where are we now. The question is, "Where do we go from here?" Where do we want to go and how do we get there? Those are the questions that we seem to be avoiding.

If history is not to repeat itself, then African Americans must arm themselves with the fear (reverence) of God, Self-Confidence, Self-Motivation, Self -Respect, Self-Control, Self-Reliance and Education. However, we must also face the grim reality that there are those who have found a comfort zone in the "wilderness" and therefore, have no desire to leave. As for racism, I believe the most effective way to combat this evil is to take full advantage of the sacrifices (blood, sweat, and tears) made by our ancestors. Until we do that, we can march, protest, cast blame, enact laws, offer free education, etc., but only those willing to come out of the wilderness will do so.

40

In Memory Of Joan

It was the end of January 2002 that I decided to write four articles for Black History Month. I contacted the Atkinson County Citizen newspaper and Joan answered the phone. After identifying myself, I asked the cost to have four articles published and she either said $40, or I offered to give that amount (can't remember exactly how the conversation went but I do know that I paid the cost of submitting a 4-week ad). While writing my fourth and last article for Black History Month, I received notice that my foster sister had died from complications due to AIDS. She was also addicted to crack (cocaine). It was at that moment when I got this incredible urge to write, informing the public about the crack epidemic that was affecting (primary) the black community…but the nation as well. Having been addicted to crack, I felt that I could bring the reader into the mind of the crack addict if I could share with the public my experience with crack.

A week following the memorial service for my foster sister, I contacted Joan again and told her I would be sending another $40 to have four more articles published. To my total amazement she said, "We won't charge you anything. Just write for us. We can't pay you but we would be glad to have you write for us." I was very grateful and thanked her but did have one stipulation. I said to her, "Just put my picture in the paper." (I can't believe I just admitted that but I did apologize to Joan two years later for making such a vain request. She just laughed it off and said she didn't think anything of it). I also told her that I would like for my articles to written under the theme, "My View."

After I'd written approximately 40 articles about my crack addiction and recovery, breaking occasionally to write about other things, I decided that I did not want to write anymore. Not only was writing weekly articles taxing but I had told my story and therefore, had nothing else "safe" to write about; therefore, approximately one year after submitting my first article the ACC, I informed Joan (in an email) that I would no longer be writing and I thanked her for giving me the opportunity to share my story with the public. She did not reply. In July 2004, I was approached by a black gentleman in the community and encouraged to resume writing because as he put it," We need a black voice in Atkinson County." I thought about it for a week or two before contacting Joan (by phone) and telling her I wanted to resume writing. She stated, "Well, I hated it when you stopped [writing] but I understood. We missed you."

I wasn't exactly sure what having "A black voice" in Atkinson County meant but my articles would not be about slavery or racism…but rather how to overcome those evils.

The first year I resumed writing, I often held my breath… only to breathe a sigh of relief when my articles were published. I did not discriminate when it came to expressing my view, whether I was writing about black-on-black crime, or the Confederate flag. Although several of my articles were controversial, Joan never refused to publish anything I submitted. However, if she did not agree with something I'd written, she would email me, expressing how she felt. By doing so, she helped me to focus more, not only on what I was writing (the content) but also how I was writing it. She had a way of correcting me without making me feel as if I'd done something wrong. I perceived her to be fair when it came to the issue of race relations; therefore, I valued her opinion. I never knew her to take sides with anyone…unless she felt the other party was wrong.

Joan and I met face to face only four or five times during the many years I knew her but we would communicate at least three or four times a year via phone, email, or social media. When her mother passed, she shared with me some of the things she was experiencing, which were not unlike what I had experienced after the death of my father. These are things one does not share with just anybody and I think she found great comfort in knowing that she was not alone.

When it came to race relations in America, she and I shared many of the same views but because she was white, she did not make her views public…for obvious reasons. But I was able to look beyond the color of her skin and see the person within and what I saw was a good heart. I can't speak for anyone else, nor do I desire to but for me…she was a friend. On April 24, 2014 at 9:37 pm, she sent me the following message:

Joan: *"Harvey, I have been called by the Lord to write a Blog to inspire and encourage people in their walk with God. But not being as gifted a writer as you I wonder if you would mind reading some of [my] writings and let me know what you think. If you don't mind, send me your email address and I will forward it on to you. Any help would be greatly appreciated."*

Not only did she believe in me, she encouraged me in ways she probably never even knew. Here you have the editor of a newspaper asking "me" to critique her writing. Any doubt I may have had as a writer, I had to abandon because she was depending on me to help her. Like everybody else, Joan had her enemies too. Here's another message she sent to me on August 23, 2011 at 10:54 am via FB:

Joan: *"Thanks for your prayers. God knows I need them right now. I know the one true God and I know he will take care of the ones who wish to do me harm. I also know that while man's words hurt, God's words and promises are the only true words and the only ones that I should cling to. That said please keep me, the newspaper and my family in you prayers as the devil's helpers are out & running. As for the coin articles, I think they will be an interesting addition. Maybe twice a month. Explaining coin collecting, certain coins, how to get started etc."*

Harvey: *"Yes, I will definitely keep you in prayer. The devil ALWAYS chooses good people to attack but God protects His sheep. Believe me, I have my share of enemies too. I have to REALLY pray to love those people as I do everyone else. Some people are just wrongdoers but then some are downright EVIL. The evil ones make it a mission to destroy your reputation & good standing in the community but I leave them to God! As for the Coin Articles, Thanks. I would like to do it just when I'm* *in the mood, which will be at least once a month. I really want to do it for the kids and the articles will be short. I had quite a few adults that were interested in the past coin articles as well. Again, I DEEPLY appreciates you providing me an avenue to express my thoughts and feeling regarding certain issues. If I can EVER be of any help to you, Please, do not hesitate to contact me. I will continue to pray for you, your family, paper, staff, etc. Love, Harvey"*

Joan was also a supporter of the MLK Day Celebration. In fact, the first time I actually sat down and talked with her face to face was at a MLK Breakfast in Willacoochee. Last year she could not be there but sent the following message on January 20, 2014 at 9:16 pm via FB:

Joan: *"Harvey, can you send me a write up and a few pics from today and Sunday. Rob was sick and did not get to go and I did not have the camera. Plus being the only one in the office, I needed to keep it open. Thanks in advance. Joan"*

As I've said so many times in the past, *"Love and friendship does not recognize race or color."* In my eyes, Joan was a prime example. When I solicited funds on FB last year to help a local child battling a rare blood disease, Joan sent the following message on August 13, 2014 at 12:07 pm via FB:

Joan: *"I would love to [do a] story on _____ in the paper if his family is open to it. Can you check with them and get back with me."*

Harvey: "Hi Joan, the family has given permission to do a story on _____."

Joan: *"Great!!! I will get with Blake and get him with you to set up a meeting."*

I didn't know it at the time but this would be the last time Joan and I would communication on this side of Heaven. I knew that she was sick but didn't know the extent of her illness. On December 31, 2014 at 10:08 pm I took a chance and sent her the following message via FB:

Harvey: How are you? Been thinking about you.

When I received no reply, I knew her condition was serious and I prayed that God would raise her up but apparently, He said, "No. Not on this side." I was unaware that she had passed on Monday, when I asked the church on Wednesday to pray for her. Nevertheless, Joan managed to bless me one last time when the casket was opened for final viewing at the memorial service. I wanted to look upon her face one more time and I was blessed to do just that. Rest In Peace, My Dear Friend…and Thanks Again!

Joan LaRita Vickers (July 17, 1963 – February 9, 2015)

Printed in the United States
By Bookmasters